A MANUAL OF
MODERN PALMISTRY

A MANUAL OF
MODERN PALMISTRY

MICHAEL P. MOORE

AURUM PRESS

First published in 1996 by Aurum Press Ltd
25 Bedford Avenue, London WC1B 3AT

A catalogue record for this book is available from the
British Library.

ISBN 1 85410 351 2

Line drawings by Jane Fallows
Book design by Judy Gordon
Printed in Lebanon

CONTENTS

INTRODUCTION	vii
WHAT IS PALMISTRY?	ix

PART I: CHIROLOGY — 1

PHYSICAL ASPECTS OF THE HAND	3
Left and Right Hands	6
The Texture of the Skin	9
The Consistency of the Hand	12
The Flexibility of the Hand	16
The Colour of the Palm	20
The Divisions of the Hand	24
The Fingers	29
The Thumb	47
THE MOUNTS OF THE HAND	61
The Mount of Jupiter	69
The Mount of Saturn	77
The Mount of Apollo	86
The Mount of Mercury	95
The Mounts of Mars	106
The Mount of Luna	114
The Mount of Venus	123
ACTIVE AND PASSIVE ZONES OF THE HAND	131
READING A DIFFICULT HAND	135
PALMISTRY ASSESSMENT FORM	137

PART II: CHIROMANCY — 141

THE LINES OF THE HAND	143
The Heart Line	147
The Head Line	157
The Life Line	170
The Fate Line	179
The Line of Apollo	192

Minor Lines of the Hand   196
COLLECTING PALM PRINTS   203
CHECK-LIST FOR LINES OF THE HAND   205

RECOMMENDED READING   207

INTRODUCTION

*P*almistry is a fascinating and exciting science which can enable you to understand the true nature of another person simply by looking at their hand. But, contrary to what many authors on the subject suggest, there is no escaping the fact that it is a complex and in-depth subject. There is no easy road to becoming a proficient palm reader and proficiency can only be attained through practice and a willingness to learn from your experiences. To avoid confusion and ensure that your learning is as logical and progressive as possible, this book is laid out on a step-by-step basis and each chapter seeks to build on the ones that have preceded it. A competent reader doesn't just look at a hand and talk about the first thing that attracts his or her attention. There is a structured way of working and each aspect of the hand has to be examined individually and in a particular sequence. By doing this the reader builds a detailed picture of the subject. Read each section of this book in sequence and you will find yourself led further and further into the many complex and fascinating aspects of palm reading.

WHAT IS PALMISTRY?

*T*he first part of this book is devoted to some general knowledge about palmistry and its surrounding environment. Most people have a very confused idea as to what palmistry actually is and what a palm reader can and cannot do. They read articles in magazines and the popular press, listen to the claims of charlatans, hear stories concerning incredible predictions and then, not surprisingly, formulate opinions that are hopelessly unrealistic.

Palmistry is, in reality, nothing more than a form of diagnosis. The palmist of today (a genuine one) looks at the hands of his or her subject and, through a careful and systematic analysis of as many aspects of those hands as possible, seeks to determine the nature of the subject's character, psychology, general health, personality and course through life. Every hand tells its own story. But there are limits, and any reader who claims to be able to predict a client's marriage, how long they will live or how successful they will be is not a genuine palm reader.

▶ Palm Readers, Card Readers, Clairvoyants, and Charlatans

There is a big difference between knowing something about palmistry and actually applying your knowledge by reading somebody's hands. How you deal with your subject is of the utmost importance, and having a good general knowledge about all

aspects relating to this field will benefit you greatly
– as not only will you be able to handle questions
that relate to the reading you are doing, you will
also be able to deal with any queries concerning the
difference between what you have just said and
what a reader they visited last week/month/year
said. If they went to a scientific hand analyst then
the chances are that you will have both said much
the same thing. But if they went to a tarot reader,
psychic, clairvoyant palm reader, or charlatan you
will have to be able to explain why what you said
was so different to what they were told last time. By
knowing something about other types of readers
you will be more able to handle the various kinds of
questions a client is likely to ask you.

A technical palm reader or scientific hand analyst
determines everything they say from an inspection
of various aspects of the hand. They may, from time
to time, make an educated guess based on a variety of
factors in the hands they are studying, but they
never, ever, say anything just because it's a gut
feeling or an idea that happened to pop into their
head. If asked, they are able to clarify each and every
statement they made and point out the lines or marks
on the hand that led to a particular conclusion.

Psychics or clairvoyant palm readers call themselves palmists but may know little or nothing about
the actual science of palmistry. The person's palm is
a focal point or medium for their abilities and by
using their intuition they are able to make incidental
or short-term predictions regarding the client's
immediate future. The problem is that someone who
has been to a clairvoyant palm reader in the past is
often unable to understand why every palmist
cannot do the same sort of work. The scientific hand
analyst then has to explain the difference between
the two types of readings and (usually) why they are
unable to make any comments on an incidental
matter that might presently be troubling their client.

A card reader is one who seeks to foretell the

future by using a pack of playing cards, or, more commonly, a pack of specially designed tarot cards. By getting the client to shuffle and cut the cards and then dealing them out in any one of a number of mystic layouts, he or she will use them as a medium for foretelling their subject's future. Some readers stick rigidly to the standard interpretations of the cards that are dealt out while others use their intuition or gut feeling and say whatever comes into their head. The type of predictions a tarot reader makes are generally short term and often incidental to the overall course of a subject's life.

The psychic is similar to the card reader and also usually deals in incidental or short-term predictions. He usually works by responding to the feelings or ideas he gets while looking at his client or holding a personal possession which belongs either to the subject or to some other person the subject is interested in finding out about.

Astrologers believe that the planets in the solar system affect much of what happens on Earth and a competent astrologer is very scientific and mathematical in the way he approaches his work. Popular astrology as generally found in newspapers and women's magazines does little more than make life difficult for genuine astrologers. Articles on astrology sell magazines and editors generally prefer to cater to the whims of their readers rather than to the scientific realities of genuine astrology.

A charlatan is a reader who does not deceive himself. Generally good with words and smooth talkers, charlatans will set themselves up as palmists, clairvoyants, or other forms of fortune tellers with the express intention of defrauding their customers – a job made considerably easier by the general public's lack of knowledge and their anxiety to know what the future holds. There are a wide variety of subtle tricks that enable charlatans to put their clients at a severe psychological disadvantage and, provided they are careful in their use of words

and choice of victim, they have a very good chance
of never being found out.

Some time ago an American professor of psychology explained how easy it was for a dishonest
person to pass himself off as a palm reader. When a
person who is having his palm read is interested in
what the reader is saying he unintentionally pushes
his hands closer to the reader. When he is not interested in what is being said his instinct is to pull his
hands away. So, by saying the first plausible thing
that comes into his head, the charlatan can be
guided by the way a subject's hands move.

▶ Can the Hand really Foretell the Future?

The whole question of predicting the future by
reading a person's palm is highly controversial and
often leads to intense argument or debate. Some
people believe that the hand *can* foretell the future
while others find such an idea outrageous and
refuse even to consider the possibility. Few are
open-minded enough to weigh both sides of the
question and approach the subject in a practical and
objective way.

The surprising thing is, however, that in most
walks of life forecasting the future is an everyday
occurrence. A timetable of any sort is unquestion-
ably an attempt to foretell or predict the future.
(The train leaving station A at 9.00 am will arrive at
station B at such and such a time.) Provided the
person who draws up the timetable is accurately
informed of all the necessary data, that particular
timetable for future events can be expected to be
accurate and will be relied on by those who use the
service.

In medicine, if a patient has a fatal form of cancer
a doctor can usually foretell with a reasonable
degree of accuracy when the patient is likely to die.

The more the doctor knows about that particular form of cancer and its effect on the body, the more accurate the predictions are likely to be. A heavy smoker who has a high cholesterol level and a sedentary occupation can be expected to have heart trouble at some time in the future. When this may occur will depend on a variety of factors but an astute doctor could more than likely make an accurate assessment as to the possible age bracket.

And so it is with palmistry. Except that when we deal with the life of an individual we are dealing with the human brain, something which is infinitely more complex and vastly superior to even the world's biggest and most advanced computer. Part of the brain is a recording device which records everything an individual has ever experienced. It also records the details of how he reacts to each experience and the effect of that experience on his decision-making processes. Even more importantly, the brain is fully aware of everything about its owner: his innermost nature, his psychology, his likes, dislikes, fears, dreams, and hopes. It is also very aware of the environment in which the individual lives and consequently, if asked, it would easily anticipate the future of its owner for any particular year with an extremely high degree of accuracy.

The hand is the servant of the brain and, therefore, the place where the brain prints out its expectations of future trends in a code which can be read by anyone who takes the trouble to learn to understand it.

Some people argue that because lines on the hand have been known to change this negates the predictive value of palmistry. It is true that lines do change. If somebody undergoes a change in his nature then his attitude to life will alter, the type of decisions he makes will change, and this will more than likely result in a change or alteration to the expected trend of his life. Changing lines are, however, a very unusual occurrence. When there is an alteration, future trends shown before the change are not always the same as those shown afterwards. But this is easily explained by the individual undergoing any change in his inner nature that had not previously been anticipated by the brain. The brain may have been aware that, given a particular influence or event, it would start reacting differently to certain stimuli and this would result in a need to modify its assessment of future trends. But although it was aware of this possibility, it may, taking everything into consideration, have perceived that such an influence or event was highly unlikely. It therefore assessed the probability of future trends on the assumption that such an influence or event would not occur. When the influence or event did occur and it suddenly started reacting differently to certain inputs, its assessment of future trends would have automatically undergone a change and this would then have been reflected by a modification to the lines on the hand.

It is important to remember this point when reading a palm and dealing with the future events of your subject's life. Because something is marked in the hand it is not a guarantee that it will come to pass. Although the mark will indicate what the brain presently anticipates for the future, there is always a possibility that something will occur to modify or change the expected course of events.

▶ Becoming a Proficient Palm Reader

Your first step to attaining proficiency as a palm reader is to get the basics fixed in your mind and to do each reading according to a set procedure. After that, developing and refining your skills will simply be a matter of continual practice.

The structure of learning and reading hands laid out in this book is based on the most solid foundations. It is specially designed to guide you through the learning processes and to show you how to read palms. As you progress and develop your skills you will obviously insert your personality into your readings and do things in your own way. But by following the concepts laid out in this book, your method of working will always be constructive and progressive.

Being positive about what you say when reading palms is important. When you find negative indications you should always encourage your subject to seek professional help. A palmist is a diagnostician, not a doctor, psychologist nor consultant psychiatrist. Their job is to diagnose, not to cure. Although a palm reader can warn people of impending difficulties, most will ignore the warnings because they are being influenced by what their subconscious mind wants.* A warning is often not enough to forestall an impending disaster and this is why, when lines relating to future probabilities are poorly marked or show negative trends, the client should be advised to seek professional help from a trained psychologist or psychiatrist. Remember that a palm reader is not trained in the intricacies of psychological treatment and is also not in a position to give his subject the continued help, support, and encouragement he needs to make any necessary changes. The greater your understanding of human nature, psychology, and medicine, the greater your chances of becoming a proficient reader. Being able to foretell the likely course of a person's life is one thing; being able to understand why he is likely to take such a course in life is the mark of a really competent palm reader.

* See Eric Berne, *What Do You Say After You Say Hello?* (Corgi Books, London, 1988) and *A Layman's Guide to Psychiatry and Psychoanalysis* (Penguin Books, London, 1986).

PART I
CHIROLOGY

PHYSICAL ASPECTS
OF THE HAND

*C*hirology is the study of the physical aspects of
the hand and deals with such things as the
colour of the palm, the lengths of the fingers, the
shape of the fingertips, the thumb, and the mounts
on the hand. This has little to do with the lines
found on the hand or an individual's course through
life. Unfortunately, many students are so keen to
study the lines and look at future probabilities that
they fail to pay enough attention to this most
important aspect of hand reading. Yet an accurate
and in-depth reading of the lines depends on the
reader having a good understanding of the subject's
nature and character, an understanding that can
only be gained through chirology.

Before you start, however, some points do need
to be cleared up. Most authors of palmistry, even
the best of them, generally give their readers a
single option in many aspects of hand analysis and
talk in terms of an either/or situation. For example,
fingers are described as being either long or short in
proportion to the hand. Nothing is ever said about
medium-length fingers, and I have often heard
students complain that trying to decide whether
fingers are long or short caused great confusion.

A well-balanced hand is always the ideal in palmistry, but it rarely actually occurs. I have therefore
divided most physical aspects of the hand into five
grades. For example, when dealing with the length
of the fingers the divisions are: very long, long,
medium, short, and very short. This way there will

be no need for you to be afraid of classifying a finger's length. Proportion is, however, always important and good judgment must be constantly cultivated. But as you develop an eye for the various aspects of hand reading, it won't be long before you will be able to assess each point quickly and classify it accurately.

In order that you know what to expect before launching yourself headlong into the study of chirology, here is a brief outline of the aspects dealt with in this part of the book.

• Left and right hands: Indicate whether or not the pressures and influences on the subject have caused his character to undergo fundamental changes.
• Skin texture: An individual's innate degree of refinement can be gauged by looking at the quality of the skin on the back of the hand. This is one point of palmistry you will be able to read on almost every person you meet.
• Consistency of the hand: Indicates the energy levels of an individual and is read by feeling the hand and noting its degree of elasticity.
• Flexibility of the hand: Indicates the degree of mental flexibility and the ability of an individual to adapt his mind to new ideas and changing circumstances.
• Colour of the palm: It indicates the warmth and vitality of your subject.
• The divisions of the hand: Reveal whether your subject is most inclined to be idealistic (interested in intellectual matters), practical (interested in worldly matters such as business or politics), or physical (interested in food, sex or other forms of self-indulgence).
• Fingernails: The subject of nails is covered only briefly and is restricted to points you are likely to see frequently. Obscure medical indications which you are seldom likely to encounter have been omitted.

- Finger lengths: This deals with the degree of intellectual detail your subject is likely to involve himself with.
- Finger knots: Covers smooth or knotty fingers and what they indicate about a person's thinking processes.
- Finger phalanges: This deals with the areas of life a person's mind is most concerned with.
- The shape of the fingertips and palm: Reveals an individual's mental outlook.
- Finger spacings: Indicate the individual's current psychological state.
- The thumb: Provides a clear insight into the strength and character of your subject.
- The mounts of the hand: Enable you to determine what a person wants in life and their chief enjoyments.
- Active and passive zones of the hand: Enable you to determine whether a person likes to make things happen or prefers to let them happen.
- Physical assessment form: To help you note all relevant points when reading a palm.

LEFT AND RIGHT HANDS

When reading a palm the first thing you must do is establish whether your subject is left or right handed and then examine both hands before making any statement, fixing in your mind the differences between the two hands. The traditional meaning given to the two hands is that the hand that does the work, the active hand, is the one that records the present, whereas the passive hand records the qualities the subject was born with. As most people are right handed, the right hand is normally the active hand and the left the passive one; with left-handed people the situation is simply reversed.

To all intents and purposes this is still a good hypothesis upon which a palm reader can base his readings. If one were to say that the left hand shows the qualities a person was born with, then it is reasonable to assume that the left hand will remain unchanged throughout that person's life. However, lines on the passive hand do occasionally change, and the traditional interpretation of active and passive hands needs to be revised slightly. Instead of saying that passive hand indicates the qualities a person was born with, it would be better to say that it indicates the qualities and disposition he had once the psychological foundation stones of his life had been laid.

Childhood is the most formative period of our lives, and most psychologists agree that, by the decisions we make during that time and the conclusions we draw regarding ourselves and our relationship to the world, we determine the person we will eventually become. It is generally accepted that by the time we are six we have formed about eighty per cent of our personality and psychological disposition. We then attend school and begin to learn about the outside world, but at puberty we are swamped with a whole new set of feelings and we start to grow up. At puberty, we can only build on the foundations we already have, and, like it or not, the strength and stability of those foundations depends very much on the sort of childhood we experienced. We suddenly have a lot of desires we never had before and life becomes a question of not only learning to handle those desires, but also of looking towards the future and trying to find ways of satisfying them. The passive hand represents the inner, subconscious self, and indicates what we were when our biological system changed and we started experiencing the world on adult terms. The active hand, meanwhile, represents the outer, more conscious self, and indicates how we have developed from that point.

By comparing both hands you will be able to see how your subject has progressed over the years and whether he has developed in a positive or negative direction:

● If both hands are the same it indicates that your subject has tended to cruise along with the talents and disposition collected by the end of the formative period.

● If the active hand shows more negative markings than the passive one (for example, crossbars or grills) it indicates that the subject has failed to make full use of the talents and capabilities he was born with.

● If the active hand is clearer and contains more positive markings than the passive one, it shows that the subject has made a conscious effort to develop and build upon the potential he started with. Sometimes you will find this development was the result of necessity, other times a matter of the subject's own choice.

● Negative markings show that the subject is inclined to seek immediate fulfilment of his desires with little thought for the future. Positive markings

show that the subject is prepared to make constructive decisions and even sacrifices now in order to
enjoy a better future.

A change in the formation or markings in the
passive hand is extremely rare, and can only be seen
if you have kept records of previous readings.
However, if you do come across such a change, it
shows something has altered the person's inner,
subconscious being. How this occurred is difficult
to explain. It may be due to psychological therapy,
but is more likely to be the result of an extremely
traumatic external event.

THE TEXTURE OF THE SKIN

*T*he texture of the skin along with the consistency of the hand, the palm colour and the hand's flexibility provide a tremendous amount of information and are crucial to your understanding of your subject's nature. In fact, if skin texture, consistency, flexibility and colour were the limits of your knowledge, you would still be capable of doing accurate and surprisingly in-depth palm readings.

Recognizing the texture of the skin is your first major step towards becoming a palm reader. It is the quality of the skin on the back of the hand that you have to observe. At one end of the scale is skin that looks extremely rough and coarse, so much so it gives the appearance of a low-quality leather. At the other is skin as fine and delicate as a baby's. There are an endless number of variations in between these two extremes, but I have divided them into five general groups: very fine, fine, medium, coarse, and very coarse.

Gauging skin texture is really a matter of practice. Looking at hands and seeing all the differing degrees of texture is the only way to get the concept firmly fixed in your mind. The texture of the skin is your key to your subject's degree of innate refinement. The finer the texture, the more sophisticated and sensitive the person, even if other aspects of the hand show he isn't particularly able or intelligent. The coarser the texture, the more basic and down-to-earth the person's nature.

Very fine
Very fine skin texture is rare, and when you do see it you will find it most frequently on women. The skin is soft and delicate and indicates that

your subject has a refined nature and is easily
upset by anything that offends an innate sense of
sophistication.

Fine

Fine skin texture is more common and you will see
it often. It shows a well-balanced person with a
preference for matters of a refined nature. But,
unlike a subject with very fine texture, they will be
less offended and more able to cope when
confronted with a more coarse environment.

Medium

Medium texture is not often found and this is why
most authors have settled for describing skin
texture as either fine or coarse. When you see this
type of skin you will know your subject is evenly
balanced between that which is down-to-earth and
that which is sophisticated, preferring to live with a
happy balance of the two.

Coarse

Coarse texture is frequently found and easily recognizable because the skin has a real feeling of
roughness. It indicates a person who is, for the most
part, well balanced, but is inclined to be simple and
uncomplicated. There will always be a sense of
earthiness about his attitude and he will dislike
pretentious behaviour.

Very coarse

Very coarse skin texture is as rare as very fine
texture. It is easily recognizable because the skin
looks extremely rough and leathery. It is often
found on people who live a primitive life style.
People with this texture are indifferent to any form

of social sophistication or what they might consider to be pretentious behaviour. They are uncomplicated in their innate natures – in extreme cases, so down-to-earth in fact that they just cannot understand or come to grips with the complexities of modern society.

When considering skin texture and the difference between active and passive hands you should remember that the environment we live in has a great influence on personal development. Society has changed considerably during the last 100 years and the development of modern machinery has transformed the use of manual labour. One man in a mechanical digger can do in a day what 100 men with shovels used to do in a week, and the degree of refinement needed by the operator is much greater than that needed by the man who digs dirt with a shovel. As society grows and develops, people have to grow and develop with it, and a person with coarse skin texture who is thrown by circumstances into an environment which is more refined than he is, will over a period of time adapt to his surroundings and become more sophisticated. By the same token, a refined person who is forced to live in a fairly rough and ready environment will eventually become less refined. This is not to suggest that you can turn a coarse person into a refined one over the period of a single lifetime, but there will be some changes brought about by the immediate environment, and these will show in texture changes between the hands.

THE CONSISTENCY OF THE HAND

*C*onsistency is determined by taking your subject's hand in yours and then exerting a gentle pressure to see how much give or elasticity there is to the flesh. You should also ask your subject to stretch out the hands while you try pressing into the flesh of the palms with the ball of your thumbs to see how much resistance there is. If you make a point of using both methods you are unlikely to make any mistakes.

Hands can vary from being so hard that they feel like a piece of solid oak to being so soft and flabby that, as you grip the hand, the flesh feels as if it is going to ooze out between your fingers. For practical purposes I have divided hand consistency into five grades: very hard, hard, elastic, soft, and very soft. The harder the hand, the more energy a person has and the more he enjoys exerting himself and expending that energy. The softer the hand, the lower a person's degree of physical energy, and the more he enjoys taking life easy.

Very hard
Very hard hands are not frequently found. They feel rather like wood, with almost no give or elasticity. In fact you may have to exert a lot of pressure to make an indentation in the flesh. This grade of consistency indicates your subject has an excessive amount of physical energy, is extremely active and always has to be up and about doing something. Physical toil is no burden, but there is a mindlessness to the expenditure of energy, and the person won't stop to think of a quicker or more efficient way of doing the same job. Men who do physically demanding jobs, especially in inhospitable environ-

ments, almost invariably have very hard hands.

Hard

Hard hands are more frequently found and recognizable by the fact that when you squeeze or press the hand, it has some give or elasticity. This indicates that although your subject is energetic and inclined to exert himself physically, the energy is intelligently directed. I have seen this consistency on men who have not only held regular jobs in a physically demanding field, but who have also spent their leisure time building their own houses.

Elastic

Elastic hands are a happy medium and indicate a person who not only has a tremendous amount of physical energy, but is intelligent in the way he expends it. Such people are full of life and very active, they are generally up and about doing something, but they won't do too much, or try to cut corners and do too little. They work, rest and play in equal amounts and I have never seen this grade of consistency on anyone who wasn't successful. You will recognize an elastic hand because although it is firm to press, the flesh bounces back like high-quality rubber.

Soft

As a practising palmist you will find yourself coming across the softer grades of consistency much more frequently than the harder grades. Hard-handed people are generally too busy working or expending their energy in some way to be overly concerned with finding out about their future. Those with softer hands are more inclined to want to enjoy life and are consequently keener to find out what fate has in store for them. They do not usually want to have to exert themselves too much for their success. They enjoy luxury, and although they may want to be successful, they don't want success to deprive them of what they most enjoy – taking life easy and doing whatever it is that pleases them most. They are, however, generally more talented than their hard-handed counterparts because, not wanting to have to exert themselves too much, they are keener to use their intelligence to gain the maximum amount of success for the minimum amount of effort. Soft hands are elastic, but as you squeeze or press the hand you will note a certain softness and lack of bounce to the flesh.

Very soft
Laziness is a killer that will destroy any number of good intentions and prevent even the greatest talent from completing a task. Very soft and flabby hands are not often found, but are recognizable by the fact that when you squeeze the hand the flesh seems to ooze between your fingers. This shows a lazy person who wants to spend most of his time taking it easy, indulging his desires, and enjoying life. Indulgence need not necessarily be a physical thing. The subject may be intellectually inclined and will want to dream, read, think, and perhaps enjoy intellectual debate. But he will be too lazy to exploit this intelligence.

Oscar Wilde had very soft and flabby hands, as his biographer Hesketh Pearson records (*The Life of Oscar Wilde*, Penguin Books, 1985). Wilde was famous for his abhorrence of doing anything he didn't want to do. One of his great sayings was: 'Hard work is the last refuge of those who have nothing better to do.' Although he was noted for his brilliance and enjoyed entertaining others with his conversational abilities, he rarely worked. He only worked when he was forced to and he would dash off his plays for the money. His laziness, however, prevented him from making any real use of his great talents and today he is remembered more for his personality and the great tragedy of his life than for the few books and plays that he did write.

Consistency in the passive hand

● If the active hand is firmer or more elastic than the passive one you will know that your subject has forced himself to work and overcome an inherent laziness.

● If the active hand is softer than the passive one then you will know your subject has tended to take life easy and become lazier and less energetic.

THE FLEXIBILITY OF THE HAND

*T*he flexibility of the hand indicates the flexibility of your subject's mind and the ability to adapt to new and progressive ideas, new ways of doing things and changing circumstances. The rule for flexibility is that the more flexible the hand, the more flexible the mentality of your subject. The stiffer the hand, the more rigid and unbending the mentality.

To gauge the degree of flexibility you should hold the tips of your subject's fingers in one hand, support the wrist with the other and then exert a gentle pressure until you have bent the hand back as far as it will go.

Very flexible
Very flexible hands are so flexible that the fingers can bend right back to form a graceful arch with only minimal pressure. They indicate an extremely pliable and adaptable mind, one which is so versatile that it can change its way of looking at things with the greatest of ease. Such subjects are extremely clever, but their versatility can be their undoing. They tend to be unpredictable and need a tremendous amount of self-discipline if they are to make good use of their talents.

Flexible
Flexible hands don't have the double-jointed characteristics of a very flexible hand and consequently show a more balanced condition. Although clever, open minded, and adaptable in their mental processes, such people will not embrace new ideas before they are sure these ideas will be of benefit.

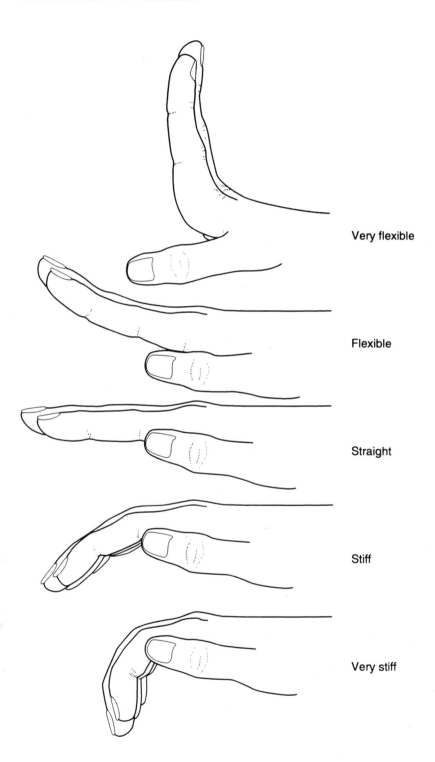

Very flexible

Flexible

Straight

Stiff

Very stiff

Straight

A straight hand is one that opens out to its fullest extent quite easily but will not bend back, even if pressure is applied. (If there is only a very slight bending the hand is still classified as straight.) A person with a straight hand has an open and straightforward mind. He takes an overall view of his life, gets on with the business of living, and doesn't go looking for new ideas or new ways of doing things. If a new idea or method that is clearly better than the one he is using does come his way, he will be willing to adapt only if he is convinced that the benefits outweigh all the trouble involved in making the change.

Stiff

A stiff hand is recognizable because when you try to stretch it out it will not open to its fullest extent. Even when you apply quite a bit of pressure to the fingertips, they retain a slight inward kink. This kink shows the subject's mind is rigid, unbendable and set in its ways. He is unable to let go of the trusted methods and values of childhood and will avoid progressive ideas and new ways of doing things, especially if life happens to be running smoothly.

Very stiff

A very stiff hand cannot be opened out to anything like a straight position. The fingers are claw-like and look as if they are trying to hold on to something and not let go. This is precisely what the subject is doing; he is holding on to what he already knows and understands and refuses even to consider anything new or progressive. He does not catch or grasp an idea easily, but he rationalizes his situation and comes to the conclusion that it isn't because he can't, but because he doesn't want to.

This person will think in the same way and do the same things day after day. A person with a stiff hand can, under pressure, be persuaded to adapt to a new or progressive idea, especially if circumstances force the situation or it can be proved that making the change will be very beneficial. But a person with a very stiff hand will be disinterested in any changes, even if they are to his advantage.

Checking the flexibility of both hands carefully will enable you to do some very accurate reading. As people grow older they change their mental attitudes and if you find the active hand is more flexible than the passive, you will know your subject has become more open-minded and adaptable over the years. Should the right hand be stiffer than the left, however, you can safely tell him that as he has grown older, he has became more rigid and fixed in both his attitudes and ideas (not an uncommon occurrence). There will be times when you find hands where one finger is flexible and the others only slightly flexible or even slightly stiff, but this is a complexity of palmistry which will be covered in the sections that deal with individual mounts.

As you gain experience in reading hands you will find various indications of palmistry tending to fall into groups. For instance, a stiff hand is generally, though not always, on the coarse side and tends to have an elastic-to-hard grade of consistency. A flexible hand will usually tend to be fine in texture with a soft grade of consistency.

THE COLOUR OF
THE PALM

*T*he colour of a person's palm can furnish you with a great deal of information about temperament. It can tell you whether a person is warm and genial, hot blooded and intense, or cold, selfish, and self-contained. There are, however, two points that always have to be remembered when dealing with this aspect of palm reading:

● Temperature strongly affects the colour of a palm, so if your subject has just come in from the cold, you will have to allow time for the body's temperature to return to normal.
● Your subject's country of origin. Colour is only a reliable indication when you are dealing with people of White European origin, as the hands of Africans, Asians and people of a different complexion do not show the same type of colour variations.

Colour variations can be subdivided into five groups: very red, red, pink, white, and very white. From time to time you will also come across yellow and blue. Occasionally, you will see a hand that is blotchy and in such a case you should select the most dominant colour. For instance, if it is red with whitish spots, the colour still qualifies as red.

Very red
A very red colour shows you are dealing with someone whose temperament tends to be extremely intense and quite excessive. The subject is unable to do things by halves and generally finds great difficulty exercising moderation. The intensity of the subject's nature and his inability to compromise will almost certainly make a normal life very

difficult as most people will find him an unpleasant companion and difficult to get along with.

Red

Red is quite frequently found and shows an ardent and intense nature – one that finds it difficult, but not impossible, to exercise moderation and has a consequent tendency to overdo things. When people with red hands love, they are passionate and intense, but, rather than attracting the object of their devotion, this intensity is sometimes more likely to frighten that person away.

Pink

Pink is the finest colour you can find on anyone's palm. While red is for heat, pink is for warmth and these subjects radiate warmth. As they are generally bright, animated and cheerful, most people find them congenial companions.

White

White is the colour of coolness and shows people who lack ardour, heat or warmth. Although they can be warm-natured, they tend to be self-contained and lukewarm. They are also selfish and will generally fail to see any reason why they should go out of their way to help or assist others. It's worth noting that dealing with selfishness in a reading is not easy as most people have a very personal idea of what constitutes generosity. It's a matter that has to be dealt with in a roundabout way because although you can't tell such subjects they are selfish, you can tell them that they don't like it when others make demands on them or ask for favours, even small ones.

Very white

A very white palm is rare and is recognized by its pallid, lifeless look. It shows a cold and icy attitude to life and other people. The person is very self-contained, dreamy, and mystical, and will not seek the company of others unless they can give him something he wants. In love he is more idealistic than passionate and even with his ideal mate, he will never express himself in an ardent or intense way.

Yellow

A yellow palm indicates a person who tends to be cranky and moody and who takes a rather pessimistic view of life. If there is only a slight tinge of yellow, then there is only a slight inclination towards these tendencies, but if the yellow is pronounced then the tendencies are much stronger. But before deciding a palm has definite traces of yellow, make sure your subject hasn't been doing something that would artificially colour the hands, such as tanning leather or using dyes.

Blue

Blue is occasionally found and indicates a sluggish circulation of the blood which is often related to a weakness of the heart. It is important to handle a person with this colour very tactfully as the last thing any palmist wants is to see a client being taken away in an ambulance.

General tips

The simplest way of grasping the idea of palm colour is to imagine a furnace and the settings of the thermostat. A very red hand indicates that the switch is set as high as it will go and the furnace produces so much heat that the environment is too hot for comfort. A red hand is like the switch being set closer to the desired level of warmth, though the environment is still a little on the hot side. With a pink hand you can imagine that the switch is set to just the right temperature to be comfortable. White indicates the switch is set too low below comfort level, while very white indicates the switch is set to as low as it can go without actually turning the furnace off.

THE DIVISIONS OF
THE HAND

When dealing with the divisions of the hand as a whole we are dealing with three separate areas of human individuality: the physical side of the person; the practical side that deals with matters relating to the outside world; and the intellectual or mental side. A lucky few have these three aspects of their being well balanced, but most people tend to lean in one direction or another and the divisions, or worlds, of the hand will tell you which.

To determine the three worlds, open the hand out to its fullest extent and mentally divide it into three parts. Keep the hand as straight as possible and don't allow a flexible hand to bend backwards.

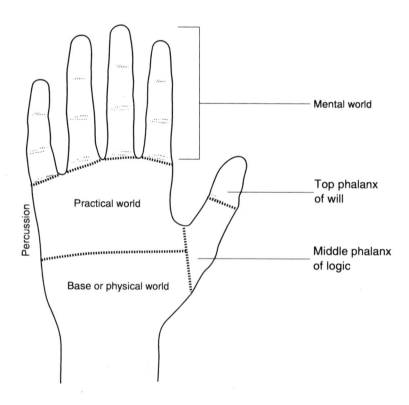

Draw one imaginary line across the hand from the base of the mount of Venus (see p. 61) to the percussion and a second across the base of the fingers. From the bottom line down to the wrist represents the physical world of the hand; from the bottom line up to the one at the base of the fingers represents the practical or outside world; and the fingers themselves represent the mental or intellectual world.

Although you will sometimes find that one world is clearly dominant, there will usually be only slight differences between the relative strengths of each world. Often you will find it very difficult to decide which one is actually the strongest and in these instances you will have to settle for an evenly balanced situation. This is a good sign and shows a subject who is likely to make a success of life. But as you gain experience and develop an eye for slight differences, you will find fewer and fewer hands falling into this category. However, it is worth noting that although this aspect of palmistry can do a lot to help you understand your subject, when reading a palm it is wise to refrain from putting too much emphasis on the differing worlds unless the differences in strength are clear and well marked.

Physical world
A dominant physical world indicates people whose sense of their existence revolves around the physical self. They live and think in terms of bodily comforts, food, home and physical pleasures. Sometimes the base of the hand is very thick, giving the hand a wedge-like appearance. When this is the case the physical world is overdeveloped and they are demanding in their desires, wanting plenty of food, drink and sex. If clever or cunning they may be successful in financial matters, but their reason for gaining money will always be to get more of

what they want. Fortunately, although a dominant physical world is often seen, an overdeveloped one is not.

Practical world

When the middle or practical world is clearly the largest it indicates your subject's main area of concern involves matters outside himself. This is often called the area of executive ability, and practical matters, such as running a business, or enjoying nice cars, or photography, are what your subject is most interested in. They are likely to have a skill, such as carpentry or engineering. If practical world people have an uninteresting job, they will spend their money on hobbies rather than on food and drink, as interests are more important than physical comforts and pleasures.

Mental world

The mental world is the world of thought and intellectual ideas. If the fingers are long and seem to dominate the hand you have a subject who lives mostly in the mind. This may be a professor, or a scientist, or just somebody who lives in the clouds and thinks a great deal. Although he is likely to be extremely intelligent, the mental nature will be so dominant that he may well be disinterested in matters concerning the outside world or the physical body, and therefore not particularly interested in using ideas to make money or get material assets. He is an intellectual and instead of stopping to turn what he already knows into some form of practical reality, he takes off on another whirl of ideas and mental concepts. If this world is overdeveloped and the physical world is underdeveloped he may well need someone to tell him it's time for dinner, or else only the starvation pains in his stomach will remind him that perhaps there's something he's forgotten!

▶ Combination Worlds

On most hands the worlds will be in some form of combination as it is rare to find a case where one completely dwarfs the other two. Each type of combination you see will tell you a great deal about where a person's main areas of interest lie. If you see a world that is small or weak in comparison to the others you will know your subject is disinterested in matters relating to that world. Here are the combinations you will come across.

Physical, practical, mental

With this combination, when the physical world is strongest, followed by the practical, and then the mental, the person's main area of concern will be his physical self and physical pleasures. The practical side of his nature will enable him to develop skills to get the money needed to pay for his physical desires. But as the mental world is weakest, this individual won't be very interested in anything of an intellectual nature.

Physical, mental, practical

Although this person will live mostly in physical terms, there is an inclination towards mental pursuits. However, the lack of a strong practical world could make it difficult to develop the money-making skills required to indulge the physical desires. Although the individual may have a job, he is likely to spend any free time either indulging his physical appetites or intellectualizing and daydreaming.

Practical, physical, mental

Your subject could be an excellent tradesman, mechanic or business person. The secondary

instinct will be to indulge the physical desires, so
that this person will enjoy work and will also enjoy
spending money on the luxuries of life.

Practical, mental, physical

Your subject's practical interests will generally be
directed towards matters requiring a high degree of
mental or intellectual ability. There are many
avenues open to someone with this combination,
including accountancy, law, and medicine. If the
physical world is underdeveloped, then the individual is likely to be the sort of person who, when
interested in what he is doing, grabs a bite to eat as
and when he can. Even sex would become a pastime
to be indulged in when he had nothing better to do.

Mental, physical, practical

Your subject will be full of thoughts, ideas and lofty
ideals. But as the practical world takes third place,
he will be unable to turn his mental talents into
skills that will earn enough money to pay for the
desired physical pleasures. This is something of a
daydreamer and although he may have a job that
enables him to use his abilities, he will be unable to
turn them to full account. You sometimes see this
combination on people who, though obviously
intelligent, surprise you by the comparatively
menial job they are doing.

Mental, practical, physical

Your subject will be very interested in mental
concepts and also have an ability to turn them to
practical account. While a person with a practical,
mental, physical combination will take a known
concept and use his mind to develop it, this person
will go out into the unknown to find an idea and
develop it along practical lines.

THE FINGERS

W e have seen that the fingers represent the mental world of the hand. In summary:

• The longer the fingers the more the mental world rules and the more the individual will intellectualize.
• The shorter the fingers, the less prominent the mental world and the less inclined the individual will be to give detailed thought to matters.
• Medium-length fingers are the most desirable as they show the mentality is evenly developed in proportion to the other aspects of an individual's nature.

▶ The Lengths of the Fingers

To gauge the lengths of the fingers, look at the hand and see whether they are long or short in proportion to the palm. Some authors give detailed instructions as to how the fingers should be measured, but I have found that, like other aspects of palmistry, it is mostly a question of developing an eye for the various lengths you will come across. I have classified finger length into five groups: very long, long, medium, short, and very short.

Very long
Very long fingers are, like other extremes, rarely found. They show an overdeveloped mentality and a person who thinks about everything. They become so mentally engrossed in their subject matter that no detail escapes attention, so much so that the person will often lose sight of the overall picture.

Long

Long fingers are quite common and indicate people who think a great deal about everything that attracts their attention. They are sensitive and prone to being suspicious of others. This sensitivity and suspicious nature spring from the fact that they notice all the little details and are easily hurt or wounded by things others consider insignificant. Although most authors attribute selfishness to long-fingered people, they are not consciously selfish. Before they give they must consider all the implications of their generosity and then, when they do decide to give, they give in small ways. People with shorter fingers often find such small acts of generosity insufficient and label them as mean or selfish, and the unfortunate outcome of this is that the long-fingered person feels hurt because his generosity has gone unappreciated.

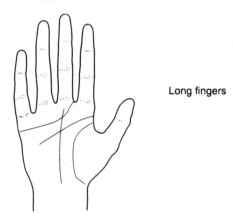

Long fingers

Medium

Medium fingers show a balanced mental approach and indicate a person who gives enough mental attention to the job in hand, but no more. There is a good balance between a desire to think about things and a desire to get things done.

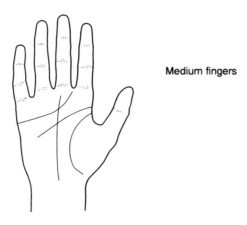

Medium fingers

Short

Short fingers indicate people with a definite dislike
of dealing with unnecessary details. They always
like to get to the point or crux of a matter and in
conversation cannot abide those who drone on and
try to cover all the details, whether necessary or not.
They are quick in making decisions and, because
their minds are not cluttered with a large number
of little details, can plan things on a large scale. The
danger is the risk of moving too quickly, overlook-
ing small but important details and consequently
bringing about their own downfall.

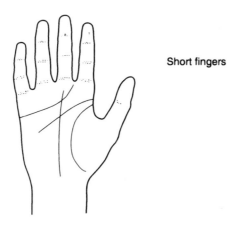

Short fingers

Very short
Very short fingers show people who have an absolute dislike of having to think about things or go into any form of detail. They are motivated mostly by instinct and always keen to get moving and get things done. When the fingers are very short the mental world is deficient, though if the practical world is well developed they will have plenty of common sense or executive ability. If, however, the physical world is strongest then they will be animalistic by nature because their mentality will not enable them to see the possibility of finding reward in something other than base, physical pleasure.

As you practise reading hands you will find that the fingers on most hands fall into the long, medium or short categories.

▶ Smooth or Knotty Fingers

Fingers can either be smooth or knotty depending on how developed the knuckle joints are.

Knotty
Developed joints or knotty fingers increase the power of the mental world and show a person who is thoughtful, analytical, neat, precise, careful, and orderly in all aspects of life. This person will want to get to the facts and to the bottom of any subject, without being rushed. And once his mind is made up, he will never swerve from that opinion.

Smooth
Smooth fingers show someone who thinks quickly and intuitively. Smooth-fingered people have a feeling for art and beauty and are spontaneous in their natures. They often make decisions based on

impulse or intuition, and are willing to take a lot for granted as this enables them to get through their day's work more easily.

Smooth fingers can and do develop knots, and although many people will give you reasons as to why this has happened (sport, karate, work, etc.), they develop as the result of a psychological change within the individual. For instance, almost everybody makes mistakes in youth, and some people, in an attempt to reduce the number of those mistakes, develop a habit of not taking anything for granted and analysing everything before they make a decision. As they develop their more analytical outlook, the joints of their fingers will consequently become more knotty. This doesn't mean to say that smooth-fingered people don't analyse things, but whereas they will only analyse things when they have to, knotty-fingered people want to analyse everything.

Smooth finger

Developed top joints

The top joints are called the knots of mental order, and when only these joints are developed it shows a person who analyses and reasons out everything that is of a mental nature. Nothing is taken for granted and every point is examined, and filed away in a well-ordered brain. This person will be both neat and precise.

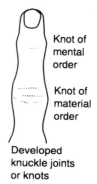

Knot of mental order

Knot of material order

Developed knuckle joints or knots

Developed middle joints

The middle joints are called the knots of material order and when only these joints are developed the person will like all material aspects of life to be neat and well ordered.

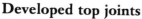

▶ The Phalanges of the Fingers

The fingers represent the mind, and the three phalanges of the fingers represent the three worlds of the mind: physical, practical, and mental.

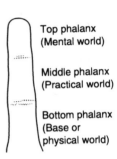

Top phalanx
(Mental world)

Middle phalanx
(Practical world)

Bottom phalanx
(Base or
physical world)

● If the bottom phalanges on all fingers are the longest then the person's mind is limited by matters that relate to his physical and personal self. This person will think about the home, pleasure, ease, and personal comforts.

● When the middle phalanges are longest the person's mind concentrates mostly on matters of a practical nature and those which relate to the outside world in some way.

● If the top phalanges are longest the person's mind is very taken up with matters of a mental or intellectual nature.

Having all phalanges of equal length is a most desirable state of affairs, but it is not unusual to find phalanges of differing lengths. For reading purposes, finger phalanges are only of real value when there are clear differences in their various lengths. If one phalanx is only slightly more developed than another, it indicates the mind is slightly more inclined to concentrate on the aspects indicated by the longer or thicker phalanx. However, if a reader gets too caught up with all the slight differences in the workings of his subject's mind he will probably end up with a bored and very confused client.

When the bottom phalanges are not only long, but also fat and puffy the person's mind is absorbed by matters regarding physical and personal pleasure, and he is a sensually indulgent person. (A fat, fleshy hand invariably has fat bottom phalanges.)

Should the bottom phalanges be long, but also narrow or waisted then, although such subjects will think a lot about sensual pleasures, they will be finicky about what they eat and the type of pleasure they indulge in.

▶ Sensitivity Droplets

If you hold the hand with the palm facing downwards you can sometimes see little pads of flesh drooping from the tips of the fingers. These are known as sensitivity droplets and they show an extremely sensitive person who feels everything keenly, and therefore will go out of his way to avoid doing anything that might hurt others or cause them pain. He is also very tactile.

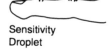

Sensitivity
Droplet

This bulging effect is generally believed to be formed by an excessive number of nerve endings on the fingertips, and the more developed the droplets, the greater the sensitivity of your subject. If there are no droplets it does not necessarily mean insensitivity, but simply that the sensitivity is not so keenly felt.

▶ Fingerprints

Fingerprints are found on the top phalanx of the fingers and it is therefore reasonable to suggest that they indicate aspects of a person's mentality. As they are formed in the womb and remain unchanged throughout life, they obviously relate to something that is fixed and does not change regardless of what happens to a person. The best theory I have heard for fingerprints is that they relate to the complexity of a person's mind. The more complex the fingerprint, the more complex the workings of his mentality. The simpler the fingerprint, the simpler and more straightforward the mentality.

▶ Nails

This section deals only with indications you are likely to see frequently. Bear in mind that nails must never be read in isolation and should be used only as a guide to confirm other aspects in the hand.

Readers who have a particular interest in this aspect of palmistry should refer to the work of Benham and Cheiro, two leading authorities, whose books (see p. 207) cover the subject in considerable detail.

Shape

● Long, narrow nails indicate a delicate constitution and an intellectual or idealistic nature. To say such subjects have a delicate constitution is not to suggest there is anything physically wrong, but simply that they lack robustness. You are unlikely to see such people doing manual labour or competing in physically strenuous sporting events.
● Broad nails show a robust constitution.
● Short nails are generally broad, and besides showing a robust constitution, they also show someone who is inclined to be argumentative.
● Very short, very broad nails show an extremely critical and pugnacious temperament. This person will argue with anyone for the sheer pleasure it gives.

Colour

● As regards the natural colour under the nails, pink is always good to find as it indicates good health.
● Blue indicates a sluggish circulation, which may be due to a weak heart, while a deep purple at the base of the nails shows some form of heart difficulty

is likely, especially if there are patches of blue in the palm.

Condition

● Nails that are flecked with little white spots show the nervous system is currently under a lot of strain.
● Fluted nails have a number of ridges running in a lengthwise direction and show a tense or nervous disposition. The greater the degree of fluting, the greater the degree of nervous tension, and in an extreme situation the nails become white and brittle, and instead of curving slightly down to protect the fingertips, they curve upwards in an arch. These extremely fluted nails show an extreme degree of nervous disorder and have often been seen on people who recently suffered a stroke or some other form of nervous illness.
● The occurrence of cross-ridges on a nail is more difficult to explain. Some authors suggest that an illness in the past caused the nail temporarily to stop growing and this left a telltale ridge which enables the palmist to tell how long ago the illness occurred. But I have observed two instances that cast some doubt on this theory. Some time ago a friend quite unexpectedly found himself under arrest for a crime he didn't commit. He was totally devastated by the turn of events and I observed that a cross-ridge appeared on the nail of the index finger on his left (passive) hand. This ridge appeared quite suddenly about a quarter of the way up the nail and was clearly visible. It gradually grew up the finger and five months later, one week after his trial had exonerated him, the ridge grew off the end of the finger and the nail returned to normal. The other instance concerned a person who had been involved in a car accident in which a passenger was killed. Just after the accident, again on the

index finger of the left hand, a cross-ridge suddenly appeared about half way up the nail.

Two observations don't prove anything, but the fact that in both cases the cross-ridge first appeared part of the way up the nail casts some doubt on the validity of the old theory. I have no new theory to put in the place of the old one, but mention these observations so that you will not be misled when reading about cross-ridges in other books.

● Heart-disease nails are frequently mentioned by other authors, but are difficult to describe. If you can find a picture of Elvis Presley that shows the back of his right hand clearly, you will see what are known as heart-disease nails. His love of junk foods and tendency to ignore his physical well-being might lead one to think that his death was to be expected. But it is important to remember that some people can subject their physical system to abuse over long periods of time without showing any ill effects, while others fall ill and find themselves bed-ridden at the slightest form of physical excess.

▶ The Shape of the Fingertips

As long ago as 1900, Benham pointed out that trying to classify the whole hand into one of seven types was a difficult thing to do, and that a greater degree of accuracy was obtainable if a reader satisfied himself with classifying only the shapes of the individual fingers. Many authors still talk in terms of hand types, and although some hands can be classified into a single type, it is wiser for the student to consider the fingers and the palm as separate entities.

As the fingers represent the mind, the shape of the fingertips indicate a person's mental outlook. There are six types of fingertip shape. Fingers can be classified into spatulate, square, rounded, conic, psychic and philosophic.

Spatulate

Spatulate fingertips are recognizable because they flare out or broaden at the tips in a shape similar to a chemist's spatula. If found on all fingers, they show people who are very active and refuse to be conventional or accept the accepted. Exponents of realism, they will always be looking for something new or different. They are explorers, adventurers and trailblazers who break with convention, have their own ideas about philosophy and the meaning of life and are religiously independent. Unfortunately, this leads some to get so carried away by their new and different ideas on God and the afterlife that they degenerate into little more than religious cranks. This type of fingertip always indicates someone who is innovative, expends a great deal of energy in the pursuit of his goals and is often ahead of his time.

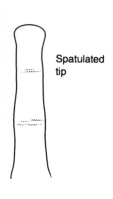

Spatulated tip

Square

Square fingertips show a person who is systematic, punctual and practical. These individuals are very conservative and resent any breaking away from tradition in case it disturbs a clockwork routine.

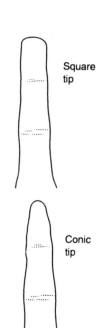

Square tip

Conic

Conic fingers are recognizable because the fingers, from base to tip, give the appearance of a cone. Sometimes you will see fingers on which only the tip is pointed, but these still qualify as conic fingers. These people are impulsive, unrealistic, emotional and easily influenced by their mood of the moment. Their mental outlook is both receptive and impractical and they find that having to do things in an orderly, systematic or regular way is boring. Idealistic in their outlook, they live for the moment, love to socialize with others and want to enjoy life. Being susceptible to their feelings they have a very

Conic tip

artistic temperament and believe that being beautiful is more important than being practical. But
although people with conic fingers have an artistic
temperament, they are not necessarily artists. Their
impulsive natures lack the plodding regularity that
gets things done and as a result they do not always
achieve a great deal.

Rounded

Rounded tips are quite common and are really a
combination of square and conic. They show that
although a person is practical in his mental outlook,
he is not tied down by a need for systems and
absolute regularity, like someone with very square
tips. The slight rounding of the tip indicates the
practical outlook is tempered by idealism and
intuition.

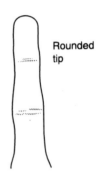

Rounded tip

Psychic

The psychic or pointed tip is one I have read a great
deal about, but rarely ever seen. It is very long and
very pointed and is best described as a very long
conic finger. The pointedness of the tips shows
great inspiration, idealism, and an impractical or
unrealistic outlook on life. The length of the fingers
indicate that the mental world is dominant and the
person is suspicious of others, extremely sensitive
and easily offended by little things. Such a combination is unfortunate from a worldly point of view
as anyone with these characteristics is unlikely to
prosper in today's world. They are beautiful
people, but the most they could hope for would be
to spend their lives living on social security or the
generosity of others.

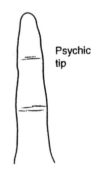

Psychic tip

Philosophic

Philosophic fingers are simply a combination of

long fingers, pointed tips and knotty joints. The long fingers show a developed mental world, the pointed tips an idealistic outlook, and the knots a habit of analysing everything. A person with these fingers reasons and analyses matters of a mental or idealistic nature, such as philosophy, theology, and the meaning of life. I have only ever seen one pair of hands in which all the fingers were philosophic.

The mixed hand

What has been called the mixed hand by other authors is really quite common. It is just a case of all the fingers on the hand having differently shaped tips. Normally the first finger is conic, the second and fourth square or rounded, and the third spatulate. This mixing shows someone with a varied outlook on life. In some matters they will be idealistic, impulsive and impractical; in others, practical and systematic; while in others still they will be original and inventive. This is an extremely versatile person who is full of general information. His varied outlook enables him to get on well with others and be good at any form of work requiring tact and diplomacy. It has been suggested that mixed fingers indicate a jack of all trades and someone who is unlikely to succeed in anything. This is generally true so long as the first finger is conic and disproportionately short in comparison to the third. When this is the case, the first finger shows that in a directional sense the person is impulsive, unrealistic and impractical, while its shortness shows a lack of self-esteem and a strong sense of inferiority. But anyone with such a varied and changeable outlook on life would find it difficult to be consistent and would consequently find any form of material success elusive.

▶ The Shape of the Palm

Whereas the fingers tell the mental outlook of a person, the shape of the palm will indicate his baser, instinctive nature.

The palm can be classified into square, rectangular, spatulate, and conic shapes.

Square

A square palm shows the person is practical, even if there are conic fingers indicating an idealistic and impulsive mental outlook.

Rectangular

A rectangular palm also shows a practical nature, but its extra length indicates that either the physical or the practical world is very developed.

Spatulate

A spatulate palm shows the instinctive nature is original and inclined to be different. Whereas spatulate fingers show a person thinks differently, a spatulate palm shows an instinctive need to buck the system and be different. If the palm is broader at the base he will be original and different in the world of ideas, as broadening at the base is the result of a developed Mount of Luna, which shows developed imaginative powers. If the broader part of the palm is at the top, the person is more interested in being different and original in practical ways, but this is because the broadening of the palm at the top will increase the area of the practical world.

Conic

Conic palms show someone who is instinctively

emotional and idealistic. Because the palm is broader at its base, the physical world is normally well developed and this shows a desire to indulge the physical or baser appetites.

Sometimes, although not actually deformed, a palm can be impossible to classify into any shape. But at present there are no clear theories about what it means when this is the case.

▶ The Finger Spacings

Finger spacings tell a great deal about a person's present psychological condition. But because you are dealing with the way the fingers are held, there is no guarantee that your subject will not change the finger poses five minutes after the reading. However, the natural stance of the fingers will not change unless there is a corresponding change in a person's psychological attitude.

Ask your subject to shake both hands a few times and then stretch them out in front of you. With the hands held in this way you must note if the fingers are held closely together, if they are widely spaced, or if one finger stands out independently from the rest.

It is not uncommon to find a wide space between the third and fourth fingers. One extreme of this pose is a little finger that looks as if it is trying to stand as far away from the rest of the fingers as possible, while the opposite extreme is a little finger that is so close to the third it looks as if it is trying to hide underneath it.

Between third and little
A very wide space between the third and little fingers shows people who desire emotional independence. They do not like being told how they

should or should not do something, nor being told what they should and should not think. They like to work things out for themselves and make their own decisions. The wider the gap, the greater the desire for emotional independence. A particularly wide gap indicates a degree of stress and tension.

Sexual problems have been attributed to this finger stance and in a way this is correct. A desire for emotional independence can lead to sexual problems, but there are reasons why people seek emotional independence. Commonly it is because, subconsciously at least, they feel that something is missing. This feeling stems from a lack of trust in others and a consequent unwillingness to become too emotionally involved. And so their relationships are unable to give them the psycho-emotional fulfilment they desire and their sex life usually fails to live up to expectation. They will then be inclined, in younger years at least, to go out looking for another partner in the hope that they will be able to find fulfilment, while still refraining from getting too emotionally involved. However, although this widely spaced little finger does show emotional and consequent sexual problems, it does not necessarily indicate a sexually promiscuous nature.

I have often seen this independently positioned little finger on difficult and troublesome children who have experienced severe emotional traumas. When seen on children it is a clear sign that they have lost their trust in their parents or guardians and are trying to handle the problems of life for themselves.

The opposite extreme is when this finger is held so close to the third or ring finger, it looks as if it is trying to hide underneath it. Such a case indicates a person who has a complete lack of emotional independence and leans heavily, perhaps too heavily, on others, his actions and behaviour tending to conform very much to what they want.

Between second and third

A wide space between the second and third fingers shows a person who dislikes formality, is Bohemian in outlook and easy to get to know.

When these two fingers are held closely together it shows concern about the future. This is not an easy person to get to know. He must be approached in a manner he considers to be respectful or correct. If he feels someone is getting too familiar, he is likely to close up and refuse to interact with that person.

Between first and second

A space between the first and second fingers shows people who are directionally independent. They are going to do what they have decided to do regardless of events or the influences of others. This doesn't mean to say they are inconsiderate, just that they will do it regardless of whether or not others will back or assist them in their endeavours. Some authors have described this pose as showing independence of thought, but I think independence of planning is more apt.

When this first finger is held very close to the second, sometimes even underneath it, it indicates a complete lack of directional independence. Such people look to others to guide them in the best way to achieve their goals and to give them support and assistance in pursuit of those goals.

People can be independent in some ways and not in others. For instance, although they may be emotionally independent and want to do things in their own way, they may still need or want others to guide them and help them succeed in their ambitions. They could be considered to be selfish as they want the help and guidance that will enable them to achieve their goals and prosper in life, but they also want to retain emotional independence.

All fingers

When all the fingers are splayed out and show wide spaces the person is very independent, entirely lacking in conventionality and very easy to get to know.

When the fingers are held very close together, there is a lack of any real intellectual independence. The person is cautious, reserved and willing to let his mind drift with the tide of popular opinion. He is also conservative, unadventurous and prone to thinking what others think he should think. However, as finger spacings show a temporary psychological condition, there is nothing to say that circumstances will not arise tomorrow that cause him to change and start thinking independently. Unfortunately, however, as we grow older we tend to become set in our ways and the habits of the past become more and more difficult to shake off.

A medium spacing between the fingers is always a good sign as it shows someone who has a reasonable degree of intellectual independence. Too much independence is as bad as not enough. Every human being has needs and if a person is too independent he will strive to sublimate those needs in order to retain his freedom.

THE THUMB

*A*ll authors agree that a careful analysis of the thumb is crucial to a complete understanding of your subject. D'Arpentigney, one of the founders of modern palmistry, said that the thumb individualizes the man and no competent palmist has had cause to disagree with this statement. Other aspects of palmistry will tell you about qualities, disposition and nature, but the thumb will give you an insight into your subject's character, the force that enables a person to go into the outside world and do something with himself and his abilities.

In palmistry the thumb is divided into three sections:

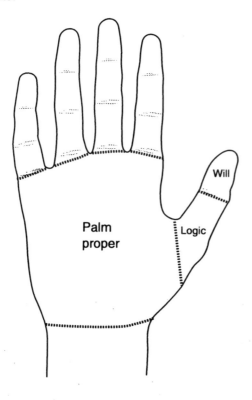

- The palm or base indicates the instinctive nature, sentiments and desires.
- The second or middle phalanx indicates the powers of logic and reason.
- The first or top phalanx is the phalanx of will or action.

Hence a desire for something (palm) is filtered through logic and reason (second phalanx) before being turned into action and reality (top phalanx).

▶ The Thumb in Proportion to the Hand

The first step is to consider the size of the thumb in proportion to the size of the hand. The larger it is, the stronger the character of the individual, the smaller the thumb, the weaker the character.

Gauging the size of the thumb in proportion to the hand is, like other aspects of palmistry, a matter of experience and developing an eye for what is and isn't proportionally well balanced. As a guide, when held alongside the hand, a medium thumb should reach the middle of the bottom phalanx of the first finger.

Large

If the thumb is large in proportion to the hand (assuming that the first and second phalanges are evenly balanced) the person has a great deal of willpower, tremendous force of character and the ability to drive and dominate both himself and others. He can force himself to keep going regardless of how tired he gets or how many obstacles arise in his path. But too much willpower can be dangerous and people have been known to drive themselves into the grave. If you liken the thumb to a locomotive, a very large thumb shows that there is more power than the person is able to use effectively – rather like an expensive, high-powered locomotive being used to pull two small carriages on a local suburban line. If the driver accidentally applies too much pressure to the accelerator the train thunders off at high speed and crashes at the next bend. The danger of a very large thumb is that its owner will spend all his time chasing one particular goal and forget that there are other, equally important aspects to life.

Medium

A medium thumb is one that looks naturally right for the hand to which it belongs. These individuals have sufficient willpower for their needs and although they can drive themselves in bursts to achieve a particular goal, they cannot become fixated on an unrealistic goal because they eventually run out of steam and are forced to stop and reconsider their position. In terms of our locomotive, a medium-sized thumb shows it's the right engine for the right job.

Small

A small thumb indicates someone who lacks character and has no willpower with which to drive or force a path forward. Whatever he decides to do, as soon as the going starts getting difficult he finds it impossible to persevere. He is ruled by sentiment and emotion, and easily controlled by those who are stronger than him. A person with a medium-sized thumb cannot be controlled by someone who is stronger than him for long, unless he chooses to be. But the person with a small thumb hasn't the moral strength to resist and, although he may put up a show of bravado, it crumbles very quickly. In terms of our locomotive again, a small thumb shows an engine that is simply not strong enough to pull its load. It handles the downhill sections easily and the flat ones with difficulty, but as soon as an uphill section is reached, it just hasn't got the power to make it to the top.

▶ The Individual Phalanges of the Thumb

Base

When the size of the palm (the base or bottom section) makes the thumb look very small on the hand it shows people who are dominated by passion and sentiment. They have no capacity to rise above their desires and sacrifice something now for a better future. Unable to resist any of the temptations that beset them, they are rather like monkeys in that if they are hungry they eat, if they want sex, and it's available, they have it. They lack personal strength and are unable to cope when difficulties arise in their path.

Middle

The middle or second phalanx indicates a person's powers of perception, reason and logic. A long second phalanx is generally a sign of intelligence as it shows a person who is capable of perceiving things and reasoning them out cleverly. The normal function of this phalanx is to filter the desires and reason out the best way of turning them into reality. Most people want a great many things in life, and their powers of reason allow them to see all the probabilities, arrange their desires in some order of priority and figure out the best way of getting as many of them as possible during the course of their lives. The longer and better formed this second phalanx, the greater their ability to perceive and reason everything out to the best long-term advantage.

Top

The first or top phalanx is the phalanx of will. The base phalanx indicated desire, then the powers of logic and reason (represented by the middle phalanx) sorted these desires into some order of preference and planned the best way of achieving them. Finally, the top phalanx represents the action phase as the person, motivated by his desires, responds to them in a manner that is dictated by his powers of logic and reason.

Comparative lengths of the phalanges

When the first phalanx is longer than the second it indicates a headstrong person. When the emotions are aroused, feelings and desires get translated into action without being properly filtered or considered by the powers of logic and reason. When angry, the inclination to act overrules perception as to the wisdom of those actions and he frequently finds himself acting in haste and regretting his actions later.

Second longer
than first

When the second phalanx is longer than the first the person has excellent powers of perception, logic and reason. The individual knows what he wants and how to get it, but lacks the strength to follow through and act on his plans. If will is much shorter than logic then he is hopelessly weak. In this case the locomotive is pointed in the right direction, the route is carefully worked out, all obstacles are considered and plans made to deal with them, but as soon as the driver presses the accelerator, nothing happens. The locomotive simply doesn't have the power to move itself along the desired route.

When considering the lengths of the phalanges it is, however, normally better to have the second phalanx slightly longer than the first. This means that logic and reason are stronger than will, and the person is not prone to unreasonable actions. I differ from most authors of palmistry in that instead of considering the mount of Venus as the bottom phalanx of the thumb (see p. 123), I consider the whole palm to indicate the desires and instinctive nature of an individual. It is logic and reason that enable a person to realize that he has desires and interrelate them with the environment in which he lives, but it is will that enables him to keep control of his instinctive desires and to act in response to his reason. A hungry monkey eats the most desirable food he can see or smell, he cannot comprehend (reason) that it may be better to ignore what is immediately present in favour of the better and more nourishing food two miles away. Reason enables a person to be discriminative.

▶ The Shapes of the Thumb

Square
A square tip to the thumb shows a person who exercises his willpower in a practical and systematic way. When seen on a small thumb it is always a good sign as it indicates the subject exercises the little willpower he has very wisely.

Conic

A conic tip indicates someone who exercises his will in an intuitive and impulsive manner. When seen, you should always reduce your estimate of the strength of the will phalanx. On a small thumb this pointed tip is a bad sign as it shows that not only is your subject hopelessly weak and unable to control his emotions, he is an easy victim for any stronger person who seeks to use or take advantage of him.

In silhouette

When looked at from the side, if the first phalanx is thin it shows a nervous disposition. If, however, the underside of the thumb has a certain bulging appearance then the person has force of character and is able to drive or force forward in life.

Bulbous phalanx

The extreme form of this bulging thumb is what is known as a bulbous thumb in which the top phalanx is thick, fat and heavy and looks like a large blob sitting on top of the second. The fact that this bulbous tip dominates the second phalanx indicates that will dominates logic. But as it lacks any real shape or form, it indicates that the passions, when aroused, are translated into action in a heavy and blunt manner. Although it has been called the murderer's thumb by some authors, not everybody with this type of thumb has a desire to club somebody to death. I have been consulted by a number of clients with bulbous thumbs and although they all had refined natures, they told me that once they got angry or upset they would say the most hurtful things they could think of, though they knew they shouldn't be saying them. A white hand is good to find with this type of thumb as it indicates the subject has a cold nature and it takes a lot to fire their passions.

From above
Look at the topside of the thumb and you will
notice that the second phalanx (of logic) is either
wasted, straight or bulging.

- A wasted phalanx shows a diplomatic person who
doesn't rub people up the wrong way and who is
sophisticated when exercising the powers of logic
and perception.
- A straight second phalanx shows someone who is
straightforward in the way he perceives and reasons
things out.
- A fat, puffy or bulging phalanx shows the person
reasons in a direct and unsubtle way. His sense of
perception is blunted and lacks the adroit, sure-
footed delicacy that comes naturally to someone
with a wasted second phalanx.

If while looking at the thumb from the top, you see
a knot between the phalanges of will and logic you
will know you are dealing with a very stubborn
person. This knot is sometimes found on people
with weak thumbs indicating that although they
have difficulty forcing themselves forward, if somebody tries to lean on or push them, they can be like
granite and absolutely immovable. It is a good sign
to find on a small thumb as it indicates someone
who is likely to succeed by dogged perseverance.

▶ **The Flexibility of the Thumb**

When dealing with the flexibility of the thumb we
are considering the flexibility of the thumb joints.
When we dealt with the flexibility of the fingers, we
talked about the flexibility of the mind and the
ability to adapt to new and different situations or
ideas. When we talk about the flexibility of the
thumb, we are talking about the flexibility of character and the ability to adapt to the environment.

Flexible top joint

When the top joint is very flexible and bends back easily, it indicates adaptability to surrounding influences. This flexibility is between the phalanges of logic and will and shows that such people may reason something out and perceive a certain course of action as being right, but if surrounding influences are not in favour of them pursuing that course of action, they can adapt and don't feel forced to follow through on their original intentions. Their flexibility allows them to get on well with others and no matter what type of people they associate with, they find it easy to adapt to their way of life and modes of behaviour. The greater the degree of flexibility, the greater their degree of adaptability. However, as action does not always follow reason, their flexibility reduces the power of their will phalanx. Although flexibility is good to find on a bulbous thumb or one which has an overlong first phalanx, it is not such a favourable indication when found on a small or weak thumb.

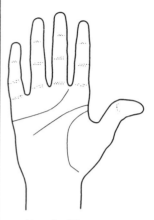

Very flexible

It may be helpful here to consider the work of one of palmistry's most famous exponents. Cheiro, the author of a number of influential books such as *Language of the Hand* (see p. 207), was a society palmist in London at the end of the nineteenth century. He wrote that a person with a flexible thumb tries to achieve his goals through dashes and spurts of brilliance. This is true because a flexible-thumbed person realizes that if his environment changes, he will change with it, so he has to dash to get things done while his environment favours his present ambitions. Cheiro and other authors also said that a flexible thumb shows a lack of moral rectitude. But such is the flexibility of their character, it's really a case of the sort of people the person happens to be associated with at the time. A slightly flexible thumb shows the person has a degree of flexibility, but he has limits and there is a point beyond which he will not go.

Stiff thumb

A stiff thumb is one that is straight and will not bend back, even when pressure is applied. This shows that there is no flexibility between action and reason. The person reasons out what is right and then does it, regardless of surrounding influences. Consequently, he is more willing to pursue an unpopular course of action than a person with a flexible thumb.

Stiff

Very stiff thumb

A very stiff thumb is one that actually has an inward kink and cannot even be straightened. This thumb shows will is bound to logic. Desire, after being filtered through logic, is then turned directly into action with absolutely no regard for outside influences. Once a person with a very stiff thumb has decided he is going to do something, nothing will cause him to deviate from his planned course of action, and if crossed he can be a very dangerous antagonist. He is simply unable to see any way but his own. Stiff fingers show a selfish nature and a stiff thumb also shows selfishness. If you find them both together you will know you are dealing with someone whose only concern is himself and whose character lacks the openness for any real form of magnanimity.

Sometimes, although the thumb shows an inward kink, it is a case of the person holding the thumb in this position rather than it being stiff and fixed. In such a case you will know that the individual has set his heart on something and has determined to do everything in his power to get it. But because the thumb isn't actually fixed, it is only a temporary psychological condition.

Flexible bottom joint

A flexible bottom joint is generally considered to

show subjects who are adaptable to their country and place of residence. Flexibility between the palm and second phalanx shows they are flexible in the way they reason their desires. If they change their country of residence, it is easy for them to adapt to new pleasures, and new ways of making money to pay for those pleasures. A flexible top joint shows adaptability between how they reason and what they do, but a flexible bottom joint shows flexibility between what they desire and how they cater to those desires.

Stiff bottom joint

When the bottom joint is stiff it indicates people who, as they have matured in life, have become fixed in their perception of what they like and enjoy. There is no flexibility between desire and logic.

▶ The Stance of the Thumb

The stance of the thumb, like the stance of the fingers, indicates aspects of a person's present psychological disposition, showing the independence of character. At one extreme is the thumb that is held as far away from the palm as possible at an angle of ninety or more degrees. At the other is the thumb that is held in on the palm and hides itself underneath the fingers. I have divided the thumb stance into four groups: very wide, medium, alongside the palm, and inside the palm.

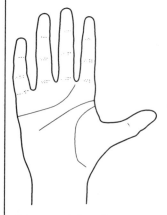

Stance of thumb

Very wide

The wider the stance of the thumb the greater the desire of the person to be independent. In a stance of ninety degrees or more the person is extremely independent, loves freedom and is intolerant of any restraint. He has to be his own person and will fly to extremes through sheer independence of spirit; he cannot be told what to do and it is impossible for anyone to manage or control him. However, such a wide stance is extreme and shows something is wrong. Although there are no clear theories on this point, I have always felt that the person is subconsciously unhappy with something about himself or his life and refuses to conform to anyone or anything until he can first sort out or fix his problem. Many people with this indication are either self-employed or hold jobs that require no commitment and which they can resign from at short notice. A wide stance to the thumb implies a flexible bottom joint and shows that willingness to adapt to changes in country or place of residence if it means retaining independence.

Medium

The happy medium is the thumb that stands at an angle of forty-five degrees as this indicates that although the person is independent, he will conform and do what he is told when he considers it wise to do so.

Alongside the palm

A thumb that sits alongside the palm shows a lack of independence. Such people are cautious and conform to the expectations of their social group. They are good at work in which they are required to follow orders, but such is their caution, it is always difficult to tell what they are thinking. They will only exert their independence when they are sure that doing so will not cause them any difficulties.

Inside the palm

A thumb that is held inside the palm and covered

by the fingers shows a complete lack of independence. Even if the thumb is strong on the hand, will and reason are not being exercised and the person conforms completely to group expectations.

▶ The Set of the Thumb

When considering the set of the thumb you must note its setting on the hand and whether that setting is high, medium or low.

Low

The lower the set of the thumb, the greater the depth of perception of the person's reasoning powers and the greater the degree of skill with which he can apply himself to his tasks.

High

The higher the set of the thumb, the closer it conforms to a monkey's hand, and although capable of doing things well, such people lack that depth of perception that would enable them to apply themselves to their tasks as skilfully as somebody with a low-set thumb. They can of course make up for this deficiency by working harder.

Medium

Medium is always best as it indicates the right depth of perception for the capabilities of the subject. Thumbs that are set very high or very low are extreme indications and, like all extreme indications, not good to find.

THE MOUNTS OF
THE HAND

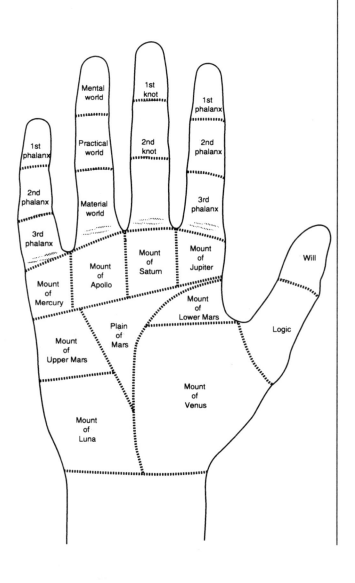

*T*o be able to tell people's degree of refinement, energy, warmth of disposition, strength of character and mental flexibility just by examining their hands is impressive. To be able to tell their mental outlook on life, their reasoning powers, and their degree of emotional independence is even more so. However, being able to pinpoint a client's inner nature, and identify the sort of things he or she enjoys doing and wants in life is something altogether different.

The study of the mounts is the hardest part of palmistry. Many readers simply don't understand their full significance while others realize that if they try to do a detailed analysis of the mounts they run the risk of making a mistake, and they don't want to take that chance when someone is paying to have their palm read. Furthermore, many people visit palm readers with a specific desire to find out about their future and are unwilling to sit through a detailed analysis of their inner nature. However, it is important to remember that an accurate analysis of the future depends heavily on the reader having a clear understanding of the client's inner nature.

Palmistry, like any other skill, takes time to develop, so don't expect the mounts on the first hand you look at to mean something to you. Learning the theory won't make you an instant palm reader any more than reading a few books on flying will make you a pilot.

There are seven mounts on the hand, each of which indicate a particular aspect of a person's nature. The job of the palm reader is to decide on the relative strength of each mount, pick the strongest, and then arrange the others into their order of prominence. Sometimes the dominant mount is so prominent that it can be recognized at a glance, but in most cases determining the dominant mount requires a careful examination of the hand. There are times when determining the dominant mount is beyond the capabilities of even the most skilled palmist, so as a beginner you should not expect to be able to isolate all the mounts in their order of prominence in more than about twenty-five per cent of the hands you examine. The section 'Reading a Difficult Hand' (p. 135) deals with some ways to help you determine the leading mount when faced with difficulties, but experience will soon improve your skill.

The seven mounts of the hand are as follows:

• Under the first or index finger is the mount of Jupiter, which indicates desire to have control over one's life and those who affect it.
• Under the second or middle finger is the mount of Saturn, which indicates desire for stability and security.
• Under the third or ring finger is the mount of Apollo, which indicates the desire to express one's individuality.
• Under the fourth or little finger is the mount of Mercury, which indicates desire to communicate.
• In the centre of the palm is the mount of Mars, which is divided into its active and passive zones: below the mount of Jupiter and inside the Life line is the mount of Lower Mars, which indicates the desire to push or force forward in life; across the plain of Mars on the percussion side of the hand (i.e. the side opposite to the thumb) is the mount of Upper Mars, which indicates the desire to stick to one's resolutions.
• At the bottom of the palm below the mount of Upper Mars is the mount of Luna, which indicates imagination and inner or passive feelings.
• At the base of the thumb is the mount of Venus, which indicates outer or more active feelings and passions.

Some authors of palmistry suggest there are more than seven mounts and say that finding a pad of

flesh in a particular place means such and such. But
a mount is more than just a pad of flesh and on all
hands the seven mounts are developed to a greater
or lesser extent. The extra mounts are simply a
displacement of one of the main mounts and
although this displacement does have a meaning,
that is no reason to classify it as a mount in its own
right.

▶ General Points on Determining the Strength of a Mount

Prominence
Mounts that are prominent are considered strong,
flat ones are ordinary, and depressions show a weakness or deficiency of the mount. Some mounts are
like hills, but although a prominent mount is strong,
it is not necessarily the dominant one.

Apex
On the mounts under the fingers there is a triangu-
lar apex to the skin pattern and when this apex is
centrally located, it adds strength to its mount. If,
however, this apex leans to one side it reduces the
strength of the mount.

Set of the finger
A finger set high on the hand increases the area
occupied by its mount and increases its strength,
while conversely a finger set low on the hand
reduces the area of the mount and also its strength.

Vertical lines
Vertical lines show positive energy flows and add
strength to the characteristics of the mount. A

single vertical line adds a lot of strength. Two lines also add strength, but less so than one. More than two lines show the positive energies are running in more than two directions and, again, are not as strong as one line. A single vertical line, if well marked, will give a flat mount equal dominance with a raised one. For instance, if the Jupiter mount is flat, but its finger is set high on the hand, its apex is centrally located and there is a single vertical line on it, it will be stronger than a raised mount, especially if that mount has a horizontal line or crossbar showing negative energy flows.

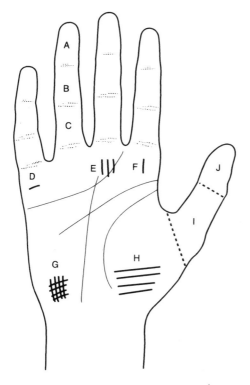

A	Mental world
B	Practical world
C	Physical world
D	Single crossbar on mount
E	Multiple upward lines on mount
F	Single upward line on mount
G	Grill
H	Multiple crossbars on mount
I	Middle phalanx
J	Top phalanx

Colour

Colour is important when considering the relative strengths of the mounts, because red on a mount will exaggerate its good or bad qualities.

Consistency

The consistency of the mount can also help you make a decision if you are having difficulty. For instance, if Upper Mars is firm but not as developed as Venus, which is soft, then Upper Mars is stronger, because its firmness shows the person expends more energy in handling difficult situations and resisting the consequent pressures than he does in responding to his sense of passion and feeling.

Straightness and strength of fingers

Whereas the mount indicates the instinctive desires of the individual, the finger shows how the mind responds to those desires. For instance, the mount of Jupiter might suggest an instinctive desire to rise in life, improve status and influence others, but the finger of Jupiter may show that this instinct is inhibited by mental doubts and a need for security. So a consideration of the finger is important. A strong, straight finger adds strength to its mount. If the finger has a lateral twist (i.e. if it twists or kinks unnaturally when the hand is laid on the table), this adds even more strength. A short, thin finger weakens the strength of its mount.

Fingertips

When considering the fingertips, a spatulate tip is strongest, square is also strong, but, unless all the fingertips are pointed, a pointed tip weakens the mount. For example, assuming all things are equal, if Jupiter has a pointed tip, Mercury and Saturn square or rounded tips and Apollo a spatulate tip, then Apollo will be the strongest of the four mounts.

Knots on the finger

Knots are simply prominent knuckle joints. A developed upper knot on only one finger adds great strength to the qualities of its mount.

Flexibility of the finger

The flexibility of the finger can also help in making a decision. If, as you look at the hand, one finger is obviously more flexible than the others, then this adds strength to the mount underneath it. Stiffness in any finger will weaken its mount.

Crossbars

Crossbars (see diagram on p. 65) show negative energy flows and are defects in the mount.

Grill pattern

Grills, showing a combination of positive and negative energy flows, indicate instability and are also defects (see diagram, p. 65). If the horizontal lines on a grill are stronger than the vertical ones, then the negative energies are strongest. If, however, the vertical lines are stronger, the positive energies will be strongest, but because they conflict with negative ones, the mount will not operate at full strength.

Excessive development of the mount

Too much of anything is as bad as not enough, and when any mount is excessively developed it indicates an imbalance. For instance, if Apollo is excessively developed it indicates an excessive and ongoing desire to express individuality and to attract the limelight. If, however, Apollo is deficient, a person will be unable to express individuality, and will shun anything that attracts even the slightest amount of attention.

Well balanced

Well balanced is always the ideal, but differentiating between the different strengths of each mount on a well-balanced hand is much more difficult than reading a strongly marked type of hand. Unfortunately for readers, although well-balanced people tend to be even tempered, more amenable to reason and broader in their views, they are unlikely to be satisfied with just being told they are well balanced.

THE MOUNT OF JUPITER

*T*he mount of Jupiter is situated under the first (index) finger of the hand.

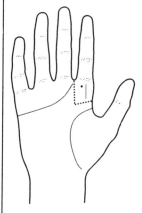

Mount of Jupiter, with apex indicated by dot in central location and single vertical line.

● If it is raised, with the apex centrally located, its area increased by the finger of Jupiter being set high on the hand, and the finger itself is strong and straight, it is a strong mount, if not the dominant one. A single vertical line adds strength. Two lines also add strength, but less so than one. A lateral twist to the finger adds great strength and often identifies it as the leading mount.

● If the mount is flat or hollow, with the apex offset to one side, its area reduced by the finger being set low on the hand and the finger itself is short or thin in proportion to the others, it is a weak or deficient mount. Crossbars or a grill pattern of lines show defects and seriously weaken its strength.

▶ The Proportional Development of the Mount

The greater the proportional strength of this mount, the greater the desire of the individual to be in a dominant position and able to control his life, situation and the people connected with that situation. The weaker the mount, the more his desires lie in other directions and the less interested he is in maintaining control over his direction in life.

Dominant

When Jupiter is the dominant mount the person is known as a Jupiterian type. From earliest childhood Jupiterians are motivated by a desire to be in control and they quickly gain experience in how to handle and utilize this control. They inevitably

develop a strong sense of status, and are constantly
looking for ways to increase both this status and the
scope of the influence they weild over others. To do
this they need to rise to a position of authority and
are always aiming to rise higher and higher. When
you see a Jupiterian hand you will know that ambition, a love of influencing or commanding others
and a desire for status are three of the leading
characteristics.

A Jupiterian is assertive, and must be careful not
to become bossy and domineering. Most young
Jupiterians go through a period of being unnecessarily assertive. Who hasn't seen the unbearably
bossy child organizing all the other children and
telling them what to do? But they learn, often
painfully, to temper their desire for dominance with
the realities of the environment in which they live.
Pride is another characteristic of the Jupiterian
type, because it is only natural for them to feel good
about themselves and their capabilities. The danger
is that as they grow older and find their status and
scope of influence increasing, their pride could turn
to vanity. However, the world needs leaders and the
Jupiterian, with his love of command, is a natural
for the job.

Overdeveloped

An excessively developed mount of Jupiter indicates that the person is power hungry and has never
learnt to temper desire with reality. He is out of
balance and spends his life looking for ways to gain
more control over his situation and all those who are
even remotely connected with it. He is a despot; a
tyrant who is never satisfied.

Well balanced

On a well-balanced Jupiterian hand the mount of
Jupiter is only slightly more dominant than the

other mounts. Such Jupiterians are realistic about their capabilities, have a strong sense of responsibility and are sensible in the way they achieve their desires. They seek to rise to a position they can handle effectively, but never try to overextend themselves.

Secondary

When Jupiter is the secondary mount it shows that Jupiterian desires take second place in the list of priorities. These Jupiterians will try to arrange their life in such a way that they can pursue their most desired objectives, while also being in a position to exercise control over their life, increase their status and influence, or direct others.

Weak

A weak Jupiter reveals those whose desire for control over their situation is low on their list of priorities – the greater prominence of other mounts shows they have a greater desire for other things in life. Although they may realize that failing to organize themselves weakens their position, they are unable to give up pursuit of their most desired objectives. This unwillingness to take control also robs them of any opportunity to develop an inner feeling of personal worth. They lack pride, have difficulty asserting themselves and are prone to feelings of inferiority. Also, unlike a Jupiterian who avoids getting involved in situations they don't think they can control, those with a weak Jupiter frequently get involved in situations that are beyond their capabilities, and unfortunately this does little more than fuel their sense of inferiority. They are inclined to lean on others in the hope that they will give them the direction they are unable to find within themselves.

Deficient

If the mount of Jupiter is deficient, it shows an aversion to taking control. Even if strong-willed, such Jupiterians shy away from anything that would require them to take charge. And, because they cannot control their personal situation or assert themselves in even the smallest way, they are, to themselves, a nobody and have strong feelings of inferiority. A willingness to accept a very low status in life and a tendency to be very conciliatory are also characteristic of this deficiency.

People either dominate or are dominated and even strong-willed people with a deficient Jupiter are unable to assert themselves enough to dominate others. Should they be independent and unwilling to allow others to dominate them, they will be forced into a position where not only do they avoid situations where they have to take some form of directional control over themselves, they also avoid situations in which others are able to control them. They are likely to be drifters and will never stay in one place long enough to become a part of the environment. Even if very intelligent, they are unable to assert their own sense of being in any society and establish a niche for themselves.

▶ **The Finger of Jupiter**

Length

- Normally the finger should reach halfway up the top phalanx of the Saturn finger.
- If it is very long, longer than Saturn, then all the Jupiterian characteristics are grossly in excess, and the person is a tyrannical ruler.
- A finger as long as Saturn also shows overdeveloped Jupiterian characteristics.
- A proportionally short or thin finger weakens the

mount and indicates the person is unlikely to be a Jupiterian.

Strength

- If the finger is straight and strong, it shows that the mind reacts naturally to the instinctive desires and that the Jupiterian qualities are operating at full strength.
- If the finger leans towards Saturn, it weakens the strength of the mount because security (Saturn) limits the way in which the mind responds to the desires. Mind inhibits instinct and mental doubts will only allow Jupiterian desires to be expressed in a secure environment. The more the finger leans towards Saturn the more the mind limits the desires.
- This feature is seen in its extreme form when the Jupiter finger clings like a vine to the Saturn finger. In this case all the Jupiterian instincts are crushed by the mental doubts of the individual. Such subjects' cautiousness or self-doubt prevents them from achieving their desires and ambitions.
- Should the finger lean away from Saturn it strengthens the power of the mount, but suggests there is a lack of caution in the way the mind works and that one day they are likely to overreach themselves and bring about their own downfall.

Proportion

- If the finger is too strong for the proportional development of the mount, then the person's mind overindulges their Jupiterian desires and they take on more and more responsibilities, even when it is unnecessary to do so.
- If the finger is short in proportion to the mount, then the mind is unable to cope fully with all the

desires and the person will want high positions but not all the responsibilities that go with them.

Lateral twist

● A lateral twist to the finger adds strength to the mount because it shows the mind is shrewd in the way it responds to the Jupiterian desires. If the finger is twisted on its axis then the person is likely to be somewhat unscrupulous in the way he promotes his ambitions and exercises control over others.

Phalanges

● A long puffy third phalanx to the finger shows the mind is limited by thoughts of personal power and sensual gratification.
● If the second phalanx is strongest, the desire for control and influence is directed towards the outside world.
● If the top phalanx is strongest, the mind directs its energies towards the mental or intellectual world.

Shape of the fingertips

● A spatulate tip to this finger, unless all tips are spatulate, is too strong and shows persons who are energetic in exercising control over others. Most people would find them unbearable, especially since, being so energetic, they would have great difficulty tempering their desire for dominance with the realities of their situation.
● A square tip is strong and shows persons who are practical in their ambitions and systematic in the way they exercise their powers of control.

• A pointed tip shows they are idealistic in their ambitions and would be more inclined to want to influence others rather than actually control or direct them.

▶ General Information

Apex

• If the apex of the mount leans towards the outside of the hand (instead of towards the Saturn finger), it increases the power of the Jupiterian desires.
• If it leans towards Saturn then the instinctive desire for control, status and authority will be subject to the desire for security. If the finger leans towards Saturn the restrictive need for security is psychological and can be altered with psychiatric treatment. But when the apex leans towards Saturn this inclination to subject the desire for dominance and control to the desire for security is instinctive and cannot be changed.

Vertical lines

• A single vertical line on the mount is very powerful, as all the Jupiterian desires are channelled into one direction.
• Two lines show two directions, and three or more lines show three or more directions and a consequent spreading of the energies over too wide an area.

Crossbars

• Crossbars on this mount show vanity, and such persons will want high positions, even if they don't

have the necessary capacity to handle them. They
will also want to get their position without working
for it or accepting all the responsibilities associated
with it.

Grill

● A grill shows an unstable condition and a dissi-
pation of the energies. Sometimes such persons will
apply themselves towards getting control of their
situation and improving their status (vertical lines),
other times they will be completely negative about
the whole issue and feel they should have a high
position regardless of whether they merit it or not
(cross-bars).

Active/passive hands

● If the mount of Jupiter is stronger and more
clearly developed in the active hand, such persons
have learnt to pay more attention to the necessities
of controlling their own situation, are more
assertive and have developed a greater sense of
pride in themselves as an individual.
● If the mount on the active hand is weaker, then
such subjects have lost their inclination to control
their destiny and do not feel as good about themselves as they used to. I have seen this change in a
number of drug addicts. But this is explained by the
fact that a strong Jupiter with a straight finger
shows they feel their direction in life is controlled
by their inner power, whereas with a weak mount
and leaning finger they feel their direction is dependent on outside influences. Once addicts become a
slave to their habit they lose their ability to control
their situation and eventually their inclination or
desire to do so.

THE MOUNT OF SATURN

*T*he Mount of Saturn is situated under the second or middle finger of the hand. A high and developed mount is a rarity, a flat one is normal, and sometimes there is even a depression.

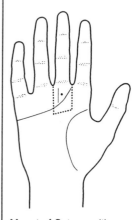

Mount of Saturn, with apex indicated by dot in central location and single vertical line.

• If the mount is clearly marked, with its apex centrally located, its area increased by the finger being set high on the hand, and the finger itself is strong and straight, it is a strong mount, if not the dominant one. A single vertical line adds great strength. Two lines also add strength but less so than one. A lateral twist to the Saturn finger also adds great strength and often identifies it as the leading mount.
• If the mount is hollow, with its apex leaning towards one side, its area reduced by the finger of Saturn being set low on the hand, and the finger itself is short or weak in proportion to the others, it is a weak or deficient mount. Crossbars or a grill show defects and weaken the relative strength of the Saturnian characteristics.

▶ The Proportional Development of the Mount

Dominant
When Saturn is the strongest mount on the hand such persons are known as a Saturnian type and their greatest desire in life is for security – personal, material and intellectual. They want to know where they stand and to have a solid foundation to all aspects of their life. Absolute security is an impossibility in such a complex world, but, although Saturnians may accept this, they constantly seek to develop the security they have and they will try to

prevent others from taking advantage of them or reducing this degree of security. They are naturally inclined to be serious about everything, suspicious of others and somewhat antisocial. There are times when people want to forget their problems and have a good time, but a Saturnian's unfortunate tendency to remind them constantly of their problems makes them seem something of a wet blanket. However, their rejection only causes pain and increases strong antisocial tendencies.

In his youth, like all other children, the Saturnian trusted his parents and those he depended on. His serious nature inclined him to believe everything he heard. But unlike other children he was deeply hurt when he discovered that many of the things he had been told turned out to be lies or half-truths. Security was important to him, and he therefore started to become cynical. The more mistakes he made due to false or insufficient data, the more inclined he was to doubt what others told him and the more he tried to find for himself the truth that would give him a solid foundation upon which to build his life. Truth is gold to a Saturnian for, no matter what happens in the world, truth always remains constant.

A Saturnian is not inclined to marry as he needs to be sure his relationship will be successful before he will make the commitment. His desire for security makes it difficult for him to accept that sometimes one should simply take the plunge and hope for the best.

Money is very important to him because it gives him the material security he desires. He works hard, is careful with what he earns and rarely spends it on simple fun. He doesn't want to gamble with what he has worked so hard to get and one of his greatest pleasures comes from getting good value for what he spends. His cautious nature means he will only invest in solid business ventures and is happier with a small secure dividend than a high insecure one.

Mysteries also appeal to him because the

uncovering of the unknown increases his sense of security. If the mental world is dominant, subjects such as science, philosophy, psychology and theology will attract his attention. Religion fascinates him because, where the afterlife is concerned, he wants the security of knowing where he stands. Instead of going to parties and generally enjoying himself, he spends his time reading, studying and thinking, and as a result he is wise and knowledgeable. However, because he has given so much thought to everything, he tends to be self-opinionated and hates being contradicted.

When you see a strong Saturnian hand you will know you are dealing with some severe characteristics and should look to other aspects of the hand for lighter things that make the person more acceptable to other people. If the Saturnian's natural antisocial tendencies remain unchecked, his consequent dislike of mankind will make it easy for him to rationalize and justify various forms of antisocial behaviour.

Overdeveloped

An excessively developed mount shows the person has all the Saturnian characteristics to an excessive degree. All he wants in life is security, be it mental, spiritual or material. He is antisocial, deeply suspicious of others, extremely miserly with money, prone to being morbid and something of a recluse.

Well balanced

When the Mount of Saturn is only slightly more dominant than the other mounts, security and stability are the greatest desires in life. But unlike a person with a strong or overdeveloped mount, such people do not pursue their desire for security to the exclusion of everything else. Once they have managed to establish a sufficient degree of security they will ease off and indulge their other desires.

Secondary

Saturn as the secondary mount shows that although security is important, there are times when such persons will risk it in order to attain a more important objective. For instance, if they are a Jupiterian they will occasionally be tempted to take a risk to increase their status or attain a higher position of authority. But, with Saturn as the secondary mount, they have to be sure their gamble will be successful before they take the chance.

Weak

A weak Saturn shows that security is not prominent on the list of priorities. Weak Saturnians will tend to be frivolous and pursue their most desired objectives with little regard for the effects their actions have on their future security.

Deficient

A deficient Mount of Saturn shows persons who are hopelessly unstable, and thoughts of the future don't even enter their head. If they do, there are so many other things that are much more important to them, they quickly forget them. Even if they are lucky and win a fortune in a lottery, they will squander the money very quickly. Lacking a desire for stability, they chase after every rainbow and spend their lives running around in circles.

▶ The Finger of Saturn

Length

Security gives people stability and the opportunity to develop their life along desired lines, so it is normal for the Saturn finger to be the longest on the hand.

- If it is very long in proportion to the other fingers, it shows the mind is taken up with ideas of security and this increases the power of the Saturn mount.
- If it is short or thin in comparison to the other fingers, then the mind cannot handle the instinctive desire for security and the person prefers to avoid thinking about his future.

Strength

- If the fingers of Jupiter and Apollo lean towards the Saturn finger, this increases the power of the Saturnian instincts because the mental awareness of a need for security limits or inhibits the mind when it considers such matters as ambition or personal expression.
- If the Saturn finger is straight and strong, the mind reacts naturally to the instinctive desire for security.
- If it leans towards Apollo, when the person thinks in terms of self-expression, he forgets the need for security.
- If it leans towards Jupiter, when thinking in terms of power and control, security and stability are forgotten.
- When the fingers of Saturn and Jupiter lean towards each other there is a blending of the desires for security and power.

Lateral twist

- A lateral twist to the finger shows a very investigative mind and adds great strength to the Saturnian qualities.

Phalanges

● A developed bottom phalanx shows the mind is limited by matters of personal and physical security and the worship of money.

● A developed second phalanx shows the mind concentrates on material security.

● A developed top phalanx shows the mind concentrates on intellectual or mental security. (He wants to be secure in the knowledge that his thoughts are right.) With a developed top phalanx, religion, theology, psychology and philosophy will be very attractive, but if there is no knot of mental order the person may be inclined to accept the thoughts and ideas of others without analysing them first.

Shape of the fingertips

● A square tip to the finger is the most common and shows the person is practical and systematic in his mental outlook on matters regarding stability and security.

● A spatulate tip adds strength to the mount and shows a very original outlook on security, with, probably, an unusual philosophy on life and original ideas about religion.

● A pointed tip weakens the strength of the Saturnian qualities because the person's mentality is idealistic and impractical in Saturnian matters.

Knot

● A knot of mental order shows someone who carefully analyses all matters of an intellectual nature. He won't be content to accept anyone else's scientific, religious or philosophic ideas before thinking them through.

▶ General Information

Apex

• If the apex of the mount leans towards Jupiter, the instinctive desire for security loses some of its power to the Jupiterian desires. The person will be more inclined to take risks in order to achieve his ambitions.

• If the apex leans towards Apollo, the instinctive desire for security loses some of its strength to the Apollonian desires.

Vertical lines

• A single vertical line on the mount shows all the person's Saturnian desires are channelled into a single direction.

• Two lines show the energies are channelled into two directions and the person wants security in two fields.

• More than two lines is quite a common occurrence and shows the person wants and works for security in many areas of life (marriage, home, family, job, money, hobbies, etc. – whatever he personally considers to be important).

Crossbars

A crossbar shows the person is negative in what he does about his stability and future security.

Grill

• A grill is an unfortunate sign on this mount as it shows a conflict between the positive and negative energies. The person is unstable because he works hard to develop his security but then throws away his hard-earned security on some whim. You often see this on people who work hard, save all their money and then go on a spending spree and find themselves broke again. Life for such people fluctuates between periods of very hard work and periods of waste. A grill on Saturn will always mitigate against the financial success of an individual because he will fluctuate between a concerned and a carefree attitude to his long-term security.

Skin texture

Skin texture should always be considered when dealing with a Saturnian type as softness reduces the severity of the person's characteristics. Coarse texture shows he will be blatantly morbid and pessimistic, but a fine texture shows he is more inclined to be blue and despondent. He will be more sophisticated in the way he expresses his depressive opinions and others will consequently find him less difficult to get on with.

Colour

- Pink or red will brighten the Saturnian up considerably and enable him to recognize that he needs to be more tolerant of other people's superficialities.
- A white hand shows he will avoid others and stick very much to himself.
- Yellow shows he will be very cranky, unsocial and almost permanently depressed, so much so that, in time, his dislike of mankind may turn to hatred.

Rings

Occasionally you will see a person wearing a ring on the Saturn finger. Unless this is worn solely for fashion purposes, it shows a person who is presently holding himself back, refusing to commit to anything of a long-term nature and thinking a lot about stability and future security.

THE MOUNT OF APOLLO

*A*pollo is situated under the third or ring finger of the hand.

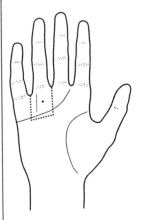

Mount of Apollo, with apex indicated by dot in central location and single vertical line.

- If the mount is raised, well marked, with its apex centrally located, its area increased by the finger being set high on the hand, and the finger itself is strong and straight, it is a strong mount if not the dominant one. A single vertical line adds strength. Two lines also add strength, but not as much as one. A raising of this mount is not crucially important because even if it is flat, it can still be the dominant one on the hand.
- If the mount is hollow, with its apex leaning to one side, its area reduced by the finger being set low on the hand, and the finger itself is short or thin in proportion to the others it is a weak or deficient mount. A crossbar or grill will also seriously weaken its strength.

Dominant

When Apollo is the strongest mount on the hand the person is known as an Apollonian type and his greatest desire in life is to express his personality and to be noticed and admired by others. This is a natural showman who likes to be stylish, has plenty of charm and is invariably pleasant.

As a child the Apollonian would have responded positively to people who noticed him and admired his charm. And, as this probably got him gifts and goodies, he would have practised and developed his powers of attraction even further.

Although he may not admit it, the Apollonian is a show-off and likes to be centre stage. He enjoys having a high profile in his community and is attracted to glamour. A nice home, good car, and elegant surroundings are all important to him, and he is drawn to ways of making large amounts of money relatively quickly so that he can afford these things. A natural businessman, he succeeds best in enterprises where his charm helps him attain his goals. Having excellent powers of presentation and knowing how to make things look good, he also makes an excellent salesman. People will buy from salesmen they like and his ability to make people like him will make it difficult for them to refuse his offers.

He has plenty of talent and is very versatile. He puts a lot of his individuality into everything he does and his powers of presentation make him a natural artist. Many other books on palmistry associate a strong Apollo with artistic skills. After all, what is art if it isn't an expression of one's own individuality and sense of beauty? And what is the point of being an artist if others don't notice, appreciate and admire the creator of such beauty? A Jupiterian feels successful when he has status and authority over others. A Saturnian feels successful when he has the security he wants. An Apollonian feels successful when others take note of his individuality and admire him for his achievements. So any artistic endeavour appeals to him – from sign writing and designing clothes to making music, writing, acting and painting.

Although not a deep or profound person, he is also attracted to the occult sciences because being able to make a great show out of only a little knowledge, he finds it easy to impress others with his skill. The Saturnian is attracted to the occult because it is shrouded in mystery. The Apollonian is attracted by the glamour and the impression his knowledge allows him to make on others. He is not necessarily a fraud, but being a showman and liking the admiration a competent practitioner attracts, it is as good a field of endeavour for him as any other.

He is a social person, a great talker and is attracted to places where people gather. When it comes to social interaction, he is a master and knows how to play the game with great skill. He notices others, admires their achievements, and flatters them; they, in turn, will do the same to him. Human interaction is an essential part of our existence and the Apollonian loves it. He is a bright, cheerful and healthy type and his ability to get on well with people generally ensures he lives a successful life.

Overdeveloped

An excessively developed mount shows the individual is driven by the need to attract as much attention to himself as he can. He has an overdeveloped concept of his individuality – which means he is distinctly big-headed, hogs the limelight, and consequently is not easy to get along with. Attaining notoriety is often easier than attaining fame, and to him notoriety may be infinitely preferable to obscurity.

Well balanced

A normal development of this mount is a very positive sign and an Apollo mount that is slightly more developed than the other mounts is good to find. The person has all the characteristics of the Apollonian type, but will only seek to have a high profile in life. Once he has done that he is able to pay attention to all the other things that are important in life.

Weak

A weak Apollo shows a person who tries to avoid being noticed because he doesn't feel comfortable when he is the centre of attention. He is inclined to retain a low profile and often goes unnoticed by others.

Deficient

A deficient Apollo suggests the person has a complete aversion to attracting attention. He finds it impossible to relax and shies away from any situation where he is denied anonymity.

▶ The Finger of Apollo

Length

- If the finger is straight and strong, it increases the power of the Apollo mount. Its straightness shows that the mind reacts naturally to the instinctive desire for self-expression.
- If it is too long, as long as or longer than the Saturn finger, then the mind is taken up with matters of individual expression and the person is a plunger or a gambler who takes chances with everything. There are two reasons for this: first, a big winner makes a big impression and attracts a lot of attention; second, winning big means having the money to enjoy himself and live a glamorous lifestyle.
- Ideally the Apollo finger should always be equal in thickness and length to the Jupiter finger, because this shows a balance between the desire for status and control and the desire for individual expression and personal acclaim.

Strength

- If the Apollo finger leans towards the Saturn finger it weakens the power of the mount and shows there is a lack of self-assurance because the person takes himself too seriously. It is very common to see this. The more the finger leans towards Saturn, the more the mentality holds back and inhibits any form of individual expression.

● You occasionally see a good Mount of Apollo
with a thin, deficient finger leaning very strongly
towards Saturn. This shows a person's openness
and individuality were crushed in early childhood.
The good mount shows the instinct or desire
to express individuality is strong, but the thin,
leaning finger shows the mind is restricting that
instinct. It is the mark of a seriously repressed
personality.

● If the finger leans away from the Saturn finger
then it adds great strength to the mount, but the
person has an overinflated idea of himself.

● If the fingers of Apollo and Saturn lean towards
each other the person has a lot of doubts about
himself, but once in a secure environment he lets go,
expresses himself and enjoys himself as much as
possible.

Lateral twist

● A lateral twist to this finger adds great strength to
the mount because the person's mind is very skilful
in promoting himself so as to attract attention and be
liked by others. It is not common to see.

Phalanges

● If the bottom phalanx is most developed then the
individual's mind is limited by matters of personal
expression and he wants to be admired for his own
physical or personal self.

● A developed middle phalanx shows he wants to
express himself in the outside world and be admired
for his work or business endeavours.

● A developed top phalanx shows he wants to
express his individuality in some intellectual way
such as writing, design, or art. You sometimes see a
very developed top phalanx on a hand that does not

have Apollo as its leading mount. In these cases you know that although the person may not be artistic, he does have a great appreciation for art and other forms of intellectual self-expression.

Shape of the fingertips

• A spatulate tip to the Apollo finger is not uncommon and adds great strength to the mount. The person is original and somewhat compulsive. This has often been called the mark of the entertainer, but if the Jupiter finger is weak and pointed it shows a lack of directional control, and the person is often overenthusiastic and apt to going too far.
• A square tip shows a practical and systematic person.
• A rounded tip indicates much the same, but the person is not tied down by a need for systems and regularity and is able to be more spontaneous.
• A pointed tip weakens the mount and shows a person who is idealistic, impulsive and impractical.

Knot

• A knot of mental order (top joint) indicates a person who analyses how to express himself in an intellectual way. This is likely to be a great talker, and maybe even a writer or an artist.
• A knot of material order (bottom joint) shows a person who analyses how to present himself in a personal or worldly way. I have seen this on people who are always exquisitely dressed.

▶ General Information

Apex

● If the apex of the mount leans towards Saturn then the instinctive desire for individual expression loses some of its strength to an instinct for security.
● If the apex leans towards Mercury then the instinctive Apollonian desires lose some of their strength to a desire for communication. I have very occasionally come across instances where there is no apex to this mount, but this is a subtlety of palmistry for which there is, as yet, no explanation.

Vertical lines

● A single vertical line adds great strength to this mount as all the energies for individual expression are channelled into one direction. In almost every case I have observed this the person has had some form of artistic occupation.
● Two vertical lines also add strength but show the energies are channelled into two directions.
● More than two lines show the energies are diversified and this weakens the mount. The more a person concentrates his energies into one direction (a single line) the more the expression of his individuality takes on a clear and recognizable form.

Crossbars

● Crossbars show negative energies and the person tends to be big-headed. He is negative in the way he expresses himself, prefers notoriety to acclaim and usually just hopes everything will turn out favourably for him.

Grill

• A grill shows a conflict between the positive and negative energy flows. The person is sometimes very positive and constructive in the way he expresses his individuality, while at other times he is very negative. Unfortunately, in these cases all gains made during positive periods are generally thrown away during the negative ones.

Star

• A star on this mount has always been described as the ultimate good mark on a person's hand, but such a mark is extremely rare and I have never actually seen one. If you see a clearly marked, well-formed star centrally located on the mount, you will know that all the person's desires for personal acclaim will be fulfilled.

Skin texture

• If the skin texture is fine the person will express himself in a refined way.

Colour

• If the palm is pink it indicates a very pleasant companion.
• If red, the person will be somewhat over-enthusiastic and a little too cheerful.
• A white hand, although rare, is not as bad to find on an Apollonian as it is on other character types. Even if cold and self-contained, their natural inclination to be pleasant will prevent them from being too cold or icy. They want others to like them.

Interestingly, I have seen many politicians who had
Jupiter and Apollo as their two most prominent
mounts. This showed not only their desire for
power and taking part in making decisions that
would affect a whole nation, but also their desire for
celebrity and personal acclaim.

THE MOUNT OF MERCURY

*T*he Mount of Mercury is situated under the fourth or little finger of the hand.

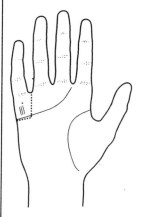

Mount of Mercury, with apex indicated by dot in central location.

● If the mount is clearly marked, with its apex centrally located, its area increased by the finger being set high on the hand, and the finger itself is strong and straight, it is a strong mount, if not the dominant one. A single vertical line adds strength. Two lines also add strength, but less so than one. A lateral twist or a kink to one of the joints of the finger will add great strength to the power of the mount and it often identifies the person as a Mercurian type.
● If the mount is poorly marked, with its apex offset towards Apollo, its area reduced by the finger being set low on the hand, and the finger itself is short or thin in proportion to the others, it is a weak or deficient mount.

Dominant

When Mercury is the strongest mount on the hand, the person is known as a Mercurian type. In Greek mythology, Mercury was the messenger of the gods and this person wants to communicate, get in touch with and delve into the inner workings of everything that attracts his attention.

Mercurians need to tune in and be a part of whatever they are doing. They are skilful and enjoy occupations or interests that test their skills either mentally or physically. A natural judge of human nature, the Mercurian understands people and knows what makes them tick. They can anticipate how others will react to any given set of circumstances. This skill has its origins in earliest childhood, when the desire to communicate led the Mercurian to observe other people and note what pleased them and what upset or angered them. As

Mercurians grow older they naturally develop their understanding of others, but they also learn how to manipulate them. Whether they do so or not depends on a variety of factors, but many Mercurians just can't help themselves.

The Mercurian is never happy with a dull occupation. He is restless, easily dissatisfied, and once he has mastered the intricacies of any subject he quickly loses interest. Mercurians have often been associated with the medical profession, because medicine is a complex subject, which, despite modern advances, still defies complete mastery. Surgery is another complex occupation associated with this type. A good operation yesterday does not guarantee its success today.

The legal profession attracts Mercurians because they love wandering through all the complex ins and outs of various laws and finding angles or loopholes that will enable them to defeat their opponents. They enjoy duelling with the opposition and trying to persuade judge and jury to see things from their clients' point of view. Acting is another attractive profession because such is the Mercurians' understanding of human nature, they enjoy the challenge of portraying a character in a fashion as true to life as possible.

Mercurians have a developed sense of judgement. They know just how much pressure is required to get the desired results, and are always delighted when they can achieve a task with a sense of finesse. However, unlike the Apollonian, they won't be particularly upset if others fail to notice their skill. In fact, they often prefer that it goes unnoticed because otherwise a guard comes up.

Of all types the Mercurian is the one most likely to turn to crime, as he finds it easy to outwit others. When somebody lays themselves open to being taken advantage of, it can be very difficult for the Mercurian to refuse the offer. How often have you heard a person say 'I would if I thought

I could get away with it'? Not only will the criminally minded Mercurian enjoy figuring out the best way of getting away with it, he will also enjoy outwitting all who would try to stop him. Even while committing a crime, he will be considering all the legal loopholes and possible options should his carefully laid plans be unexpectedly upset. However, a life of violent crime is not for him; he prefers fraud or confidence tricks and is often the rascal everybody loves. Such is his ability to communicate with his victim, he knows how to fleece him and still remain his greatest friend. He treats everybody differently because he is being the person people want him to be rather than the person he actually is.

You must look to other aspects of the hand to see what sort of intelligence backs this Mercurian desire for communication. Not all Mercurians can be high-class doctors, lawyers, nuclear physicists or even conmen. Make a special point of looking at the second phalanx of the thumb to see the subject's degree of perception and logic:

• If it is short, the desire to communicate is not backed by intelligence and the person's skills will operate in a very limited sphere.
• If long, waisted and well formed, you are dealing with an extremely astute person who, if good, will be one of the finest types you will come across, but if evil is greatly to be feared.

At one end of the dishonest Mercury spectrum is the businessman who successfully defrauds an insurance company for millions of dollars (long second phalanx). At the other is the beggar who appeals to people's sense of compassion in order to persuade them to put a coin in his bowl (short second phalanx).

Overdeveloped
An excessively developed Mercury is a rarity
because such a person would wear themselves out
in no time at all. But should you see an overdeveloped mount, the person is a natural juggler, a
compulsive manipulator, a wheeler-dealer and
someone who tries to reach into the inner workings
of everything that attracts his attention.

Well balanced
If the Mount of Mercury is only slightly more
developed than the secondary mount you will know
that your subject's greatest desire is to communicate with what he does. But as the other mount is
almost equal in strength, you will know that the two
desires are almost equally developed. For example,
if Jupiter is the secondary mount, then besides
wanting to communicate, the person also wants
status, authority, and influence over others.
Medicine is a natural for any person with this
combination because not only does its complexity
please the natural desire to delve into the inner
workings of what he is doing, it also gives influence
and status. If the situation were reversed and
Jupiter was the dominant mount with Mercury a
close second, then the desire for status and authority would be slightly greater than the desire for
communication. This doctor would be more
inclined to give up his practice of medicine for a
routine but high-status position.

Secondary
Mercury as the secondary mount also shows a
skilful person who desires to be in touch with whatever he does, but it is a secondary desire. An antique
dealer of my acquaintance finds antiques enable
him to be in touch with history, the people of the
past and the artists who created the pieces. But

much as he enjoys it, wheeling and dealing in the trade and being in touch with history is not his greatest desire in life, it's more a perk of the job.

Weak

A weak Mercury shows the person doesn't really communicate with what he does. He learns the rules and follows them. He has no instinctive feel for a situation and always needs time to think about what he is going to do. He hates being pushed or rushed and normally likes to work in his own time and avoid situations where he has to make quick decisions.

Deficient

A deficient Mercury shows there is a barrier between the person and what he does or associates with. Such persons shy away from delving into the inner workings of anything, have no feel for a situation and no instinct for the way in which it might develop. They hate having to juggle things and like everything to be simple and straightforward. They are easily confused, and are unable to keep abreast of events when things start to happen quickly. They have great difficulty in communicating with other people.

▶ The Finger of Mercury

Length

The finger of Mercury should normally reach the top joint of the Apollo finger.

- If longer than this, it increases the power of the mount
- If shorter, it reduces this power.

Strength

- A straight finger shows the mind reacts naturally to the instinctive desire for communication.
- If it leans towards Apollo, it increases the power of the Apollo mount because the mental powers of communication are inhibited by the person's desire for individual expression. In such a case, the person uses his mental powers of communication to promote and enhance his personality. He only gets involved with and seeks to master things that make him look good.
- If the finger leans away from Apollo, this greatly increases the power of the Mercurian desires.

Lateral twists

Sometimes you will see a twist to one of the joints of this finger. This greatly increases the power of the mount and when seen on an otherwise weak or deficient Mercury, the person is protected from many of the difficulties a weak Mercury might lay him open to.

- On a normal mount a twist to the top joint shows a person who is shrewd and agile in all forms of intellectual communication.
- A twist to the middle joint shows a person who delves into and communicates with matters of a practical nature. Not only is he always doing a variety of things, he is also doing them well. From his point of view, sitting down and relaxing is time wasted.
- A finger that twists on its axis shows the person is unscrupulous in the way he manipulates others and should be treated with great caution.

Flexibility

- Occasionally, when you look at the back of the

hand the flexibility of the Mercury finger gives it a character of its own. In such a case the power of the mount is greatly increased and the person is likely to be a Mercurian type.

• If the finger is stiff and has an inward kink, then the person is very rigid in his methods of communication. For instance, if as a child he was taught there was a certain way to approach others, he will never adjust to a new or different method.

Phalanges

• A developed bottom phalanx shows the person will be a moneymaker, but that his mind is limited to forms of personal and physical communication.
• A developed middle phalanx shows a willingness to communicate with the outside world. Subjects such as business, politics, law, engineering and medicine will attract this person.
• A developed top phalanx shows the person likes to communicate in a mental way and has often been associated with oratory.
• Very occasionally you will see a Mercury finger that appears to have four phalanges instead of three. However, this is only a very strong crossbar in the centre of the bottom phalanx, which makes it look as if there is an extra phalanx, and at the moment I have no reasonable explanation for such an unusual indication.

Shape of the fingertips

• A spatulate tip to this finger is a rarity, but it adds great strength to the mount and shows the person will be a powerhouse of activity and someone who never has time to rest.
• A square tip is more common and shows a person who is practical and systematic in the way he

communicates, but who has to understand the basis of what they are trying to communicate with.

● A pointed tip is often found on psychics, showing a person who is intuitive and capable of reaching out and being in touch with something vague, indefinable and esoteric.

Knots

● A knot of mental order is rare and shows the person analyses all forms of mental communication and is likely to be unbeatable in argument or debate. If he is a lawyer it will take him some time to analyse and master all the intricacies of his profession, but once he has done so he will be in a class of his own.

● A knot of material order is also quite rare, but shows the person will be neat and precise in the way he picks things to pieces and discovers how they work. It's an excellent sign to find on an engineer or architect.

● However, any knot on this finger will always slow a person down and reduce the intuitive feel for the way a situation may be developing.

Setting

Often you see a very strong finger of Mercury set slightly low on the hand. This shows that although the person has a very astute and agile mind, he isn't always able to respond instinctively to unexpected changes in a situation. He needs time to think about things and consider his options first. It is his mentality that is agile, not his instinct.

▶ General Information

Apex

● If the apex of the mount leans towards Apollo, it

strengthens the power of the Apollo mount because some of the instinctive desire for communication is given up to a desire for individual expression.
- If the apex leans towards the outside of the hand, it greatly increases the strength of the Mercurian desires.

Vertical lines

- A single vertical line increases the strength of the mount.
- Two lines also add strength, but show that the energies are channelled into two directions.
- Three or more lines are generally referred to as lines of empathy or a medical stigmata. Most authors say they show an inclination to care for others and an aptitude for a medical or caring profession. Properly speaking, however, these lines show a desire for communication in three or more fields. It is generally easiest to communicate and develop an affinity with another person when he is down, not feeling well and in need of someone to pay attention to him. Hence the fact that many people with a medical stigmata are found in a caring profession, or else are known for their willingness to give help to others in times of need. But before attributing an inclination to caring for others to this mark, check the Heart Line and be sure that the person has a naturally affectionate disposition. In such a case, you can rely on the accuracy of the traditional interpretation for this mark.

Crossbars

- Crossbars show negative energy flows. The person's natural ability to outwit others will incline him to a life of crime. If he is not an active criminal there may be many reasons to account for this, but you can be sure such thoughts are never far from his mind.

Grill

• A grill shows a conflict between positive and negative energy flows. This conflict would put the person in a difficult position because he is torn between a desire to communicate in a positive way and a negative desire to use his skills for personal gain.

Skin texture

• Fine skin texture shows that the communication skills operate in a very refined way and as a consequence the person is very diplomatic and seeks delicacy of communication.

Colour

Colour is very important to note when dealing with this type.

• If yellow, the person's natural irritability will make it difficult for him to resist the temptation to take advantage of others, especially when they make it so easy for him to do so. Once he's crossed the line between sharp business practice and actual criminal activity for the first time, it will be a lot easier for him to do it a second. The third time will be easier still, and once the downhill slide into a life of crime has begun, it will be difficult to reverse.

Consistency

• A Mercurian is naturally very active, but a hard hand shows he is extremely so. However, the hardness of his mind will dull the keenness with which he can tune into or communicate with what he is doing.

• Soft hands show he is lazy and this will reduce his inclination either to push his skills to their limit, or to try to increase them. Lazy Mercurians are attracted to non-strenuous types of work that require a high degree of skill. Dealing casino games such as blackjack falls into this category because although it is not a mentally or physically demanding occupation, it does allow plenty of scope for the dealer to increase continually the speed, smoothness, accuracy and neatness of his work.

THE MOUNTS OF MARS

*T*here are two Mounts of Mars:

● Lower Mars, which is found inside the Life Line underneath the Mount of Jupiter.
● Upper Mars, which is found on the percussion side of the hand underneath the Mount of Mercury.

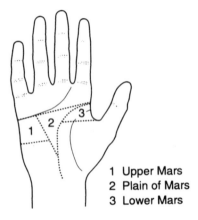

1 Upper Mars
2 Plain of Mars
3 Lower Mars

No finger is related to either of these mounts, so there are no mental qualities to consider when assessing their characteristics. But as they both have two very different meanings, I will deal with them individually at first and then in combination.

▶ The Mount of Lower Mars

There is no apex to the Mount of Lower Mars, so its relative strength must be gauged by its prominence on the hand and the individual markings that strengthen or weaken its power.

● If this area of the hand is raised in such a way that it takes a prominent position on the hand, it is a strong mount. Some books suggest it looks like a tumour and it is difficult to find a better way of describing it. A single vertical line adds strength. Two lines also add strength, but less so then one. A well-marked star, which is occasionally seen, adds considerable strength and often identifies it as the leading mount.

• If this area of the hand is flat or hollow, it can be considered a weak or deficient mount. Crossbars, a grill, or a jumble of lines running in different directions all weaken or reduce its strength.

Dominant

A dominant Mount of Lower Mars indicates the person has a strong desire to push and force a path over whatever obstacles stand in his way. There is nothing intellectual about this desire as it is an inner and energetic drive. Lower Mars has traditionally been referred to as the mount of aggression, but aggression is not a good word to use in a reading because it conjures up violent images. Using words such as forceful or pushy generally elicits a more positive response. A person with a developed Lower Mars is, however, a fighter and is attracted to occupations that will present challenges or difficulties that have to be overcome. He often wins his way through persistence and the sheer daring and audacity of his assault.

The Martian's drive naturally inclines him to shy away from easy occupations, and, often, to choose a physically demanding line of work. One client was a very good masseuse who enjoyed the physically demanding nature of her work and was noted for the way she pushed her clients into taking better care of their health. Another worked as a secretary and always worked best when there was a tremendous backlog of work to be caught up with. She was just never happy with a fair employer who only gave her a reasonable amount of work to do and would normally leave to work for somebody who only hired one secretary when he should, properly speaking, have hired two.

Overdeveloped
An overdeveloped Lower Mars is a rarity and I have never seen one. If seen it suggests an extremely forceful and aggressive individual. Always looking for something to push against, he will pick fights just to get someone to oppose him and give him an obstacle to overcome.

Well balanced
A reasonable development of this mount indicates a person who has initiative and is willing to do things for himself. It is always good to find as living a well-rounded life depends on one's ability to push oneself, one's ideas and one's plans forward.

Weak
If this area of the hand is flat it indicates that Lower Mars is weak and the person will not push himself forward. He will be unwilling to do things for himself, and less capable people will find it easy to push their way past him. While other people might push themselves forward by going to the boss to try to persuade him to see things their way, he will tend to wait until his boss notices him and asks for his ideas. Similarly, in love this individual hopes the person he likes will notice him, rather than forcing himself into view.

Deficient
A deficient Lower Mars shows someone who has a complete aversion to confronting obstacles or pushing himself forward in any way. He will try to

avoid difficulties, but when they become unavoidable, he simply stops and gives up. If he has a good Apollo, he will be a nice but self-effacing person, who will depend heavily on family and close friends.

Fingers

Fingers are important to note when this mount is developed.

- If the fingers are long, showing the mental world is dominant, the person will be an intellectual fighter.
- Short fingers, showing an impetuous nature, are not always good to find with a strong Lower Mars as the person will need a great deal of self-control to keep his pushiness in check.

Divisions of the hand

- If the practical world of the hand is most developed, the person will fight to succeed. As a salesperson he will push hard and fight to get his customer to sign the order form. As a racing driver he will push the car to its limits and drive as fast as he can.
- If the physical world is dominant, the person will be more willing to resort to physical aggression to achieve an objective.

Thumb

- Will stronger than reason is also a bad sign to find if this mount is well developed, because headstrong characteristics don't go well with the person's desire to push hard against any obstacles that stand in his way.

Skin texture

• Coarse skin texture shows a lack of refinement that inclines an individual to be more brutal. He will be unable to appreciate the sensitivities of other people and will push his plans and ideas forward without any real consideration for their feelings.

▶ **The Mount of Upper Mars**

There is no apex to Upper Mars so it too must be judged by its prominence on the hand and the markings that increase or weaken its strength.

• If it is raised and makes the side of the hand bulge outwards in a curve, it can be considered a strong mount, if not the dominant one. A single vertical line will add strength. Two lines also add strength, but not as much as one.
• If it is flat or hollow and the side of the hand has an inward curve, which reduces its area, it can be considered a weak or deficient mount. A crossbar or grill will also weaken its strength.

Dominant
The characteristics of Upper Mars are very passive. Whereas Lower Mars shows active characteristics and a desire to push, Upper Mars shows a desire to resist, to hold on to one's position and not give up despite any number of difficulties. People with a dominant Upper Mars are courageous, handle pressure well and cannot be imposed upon against their will. They enjoy defending themselves and when knocked down, they immediately get up again, refusing to be discouraged.

Overdeveloped

An overdevelopment of this mount is not a good sign. There is a time when admitting defeat and conceding a point is wiser than blindly holding on and suffering unnecessary losses. In military terms, for instance, to give ground and make a tactical withdrawal is sometimes the wisest course of action. The person with an overdeveloped Upper Mars cannot admit defeat and persists despite any amount of damage being caused.

Good development

A good development of this mount is important. Everyone experiences setbacks from time to time, and if a person is not willing to accept them and continue trying to achieve his goals, he is not likely to be successful in life.

Weak

A weak mount shows the person gets discouraged easily and gives up trying as soon as things start to go wrong. It is a defeatist attitude and it's easy for this person to find excuses for not persevering.

Deficient

A deficient mount shows the person is very easily discouraged at the first sign of things not going according to plan. As a defeatist he can be talked out of anything. Holtzman calls Upper Mars the 'life instinct' and Benham says that a deficient mount is found on the hands of almost all suicides. If this mount is deficient the person has no powers of resistance, cannot cope with any form of confrontation and is unable to stand up for himself, preferring to run from difficult situations. Unfortunately suicide is, in many cases, the ultimate form of running away. These people rely heavily on the help and encouragement of family and friends, and if they don't have that support from other people, they can find life virtually impossible.

Crossbar

A crossbar weakens the strength of this mount and you occasionally find a well-developed mount with a horizontal bar running through it. If this is the case, the person's ability to stand up for himself is greatly weakened. Difficult or awkward situations cause a lot of stress and he is inclined to run away from them. However, because the mount is developed and weakened only by the presence of a crossbar, it is only in certain situations that he has difficulty. The greater the number of crossbars, the greater the number of situations he tends to run away from.

Grill

A grill shows that sometimes he can be very strong and absolutely immovable (vertical lines), while at other times he backs down at the first sign of pressure or difficulty (crossbars).

▶ The Two Mounts in Combination

• If both Upper and Lower Mars are well developed, the person is very much a Martian type. He vigorously pushes himself forward and stoutly resists the attempts of anyone to impose upon him or dislodge him from his position.

• If Lower Mars is developed and Upper Mars weak or deficient, the person is full of bluff. He vigorously tries to push his way forward, but backs down quickly when the going gets difficult or someone stands up to him.

• If Lower Mars is weak or deficient and Upper

Mars strong, the person tends not to push himself forward, but any position he does get, through luck or the help of family or friends, he holds on to. He is never pushy, but he can never be dislodged from his position.

● If both mounts are weak or deficient, it is a very unfortunate sign. Not only can the person not push himself forward, but he cannot hold on to any position he does manage to get. He is at the mercy of anyone who wants to push him around or make his life difficult, and he has great need of a supportive family environment. (If both Mounts of Mars are deficient it might be a sign of learned helplessness. Check any good textbook on basic psychology for references as to how this condition develops.)

▶ The Plain of Mars

The plain of Mars is the area that lies between the two mounts of Mars.

● It is unusual to see this area of the hand raised but if it is, it indicates that a person has a sudden temper and is inclined to make a fuss. It is important to remember that a person can be very pushy (developed Lower Mars) without necessarily being fiery or explosive.

● If there is a noticeable hollow in this part of the hand, the person rarely ever makes a fuss. It takes a great deal to get him roused and he never gets mad or blows his top, even if fully justified. If will is stronger than reason, a hollow Plain of Mars is good to find because the person's headstrong characteristics will not express themselves in his temperament. A fiery or explosive temperament coupled with headstrong characteristics would make for an extremely unpleasant person.

THE MOUNT OF LUNA

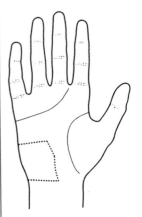

*T*he Mount of Luna is situated beneath the Mount of Upper Mars and must be judged by both the strength of the outward curve on the percussion and the size of the pad it forms on the inside of the hand.

● A raised pad with a decided outward curve to the side of the hand shows a strong, if not dominant, mount. A single vertical line adds strength. Two lines also add strength, but less so than one. Sometimes the capillary lines of the palm form a circular whorl on this mount, which adds great strength and often identifies it as the leading mount. A red patch on the hand where this mount is situated also adds great strength.

The Mount of Luna.

● If this area of the hand is flat or hollow and the percussion, instead of bulging outwards, has a distinct inward curve, which reduces the area of Luna, it can be considered a weak or deficient mount. Crossbars or a grill also weaken its positive attributes.

The Mount of Luna has traditionally been known as the mount of imagination and a wide variety of characteristics have been attributed to it. However, to tell a Lunarian that he is imaginative and likes to dream only deals with superficial characteristics and fails to reach into the basic workings of his inner self. To understand the person fully we first need to take a broader look at human nature and get a deeper understanding of what imagination is and how it develops within an individual.

Feelings are a part of any human being, but you must bear in mind that there are two sides to a person's feelings: active and passive.

● Active feelings enable a person to go out into the world and do things that make him feel good.

● Passive or inner feelings stimulate a person's brain into creating an abstract inner world into which he can withdraw when the realities of the outside world are not to his liking.

Dominant

Inner feelings are possessed by everyone to a greater or lesser extent. If Luna is the strongest mount on the hand then such persons' inner feelings are highly developed and as a consequence they live mostly in the abstract world of imagination. The sensitivity of their inner feelings mean that they are easily dissatisfied with the realities of life and they escape by withdrawing into their imagination and dreaming great dreams. However, they are not out of touch with reality because they often try to find a way of making their dreams come true. For instance, if people had been entirely satisfied with their environment they would never have looked into the sky and sought ways of joining the birds in the air. Over the centuries many tried and paid for failure with their lives, but the dreamers persisted and flight has become a standard part of modern life.

Lunarians' greatest desire is to feel good within themselves and live in a world where everything is more in keeping with what they want. As a result they are easily dissatisfied, restless and changeable. They find it difficult to settle down to a routine and always yearn for something just out of reach. They are great travellers because they often dream of living the 'perfect life', and their first inclination is to pack their bags and buy a ticket to search for this life. But reality never fully lives up to their expectations.

Socially the Lunarian is isolated. As he has such developed inner feelings, he is easily upset and very sensitive to the real or imagined slights of others. Real people are not as compliant or understanding as those in a Lunarian's imagination, and he also feels that they would laugh or sneer at him if they were to discover the true nature of the inner world he has created for himself. He is inclined to flee from others and likes to enjoy himself by himself. He is attracted to anything that gives him an inner sense of well-being and so he loves nature, the sea and the countryside. His sexual instincts are excited by what he imagines will give him pleasure but as sex is often different to how he imagines it should be, he is not a very physically sexual person. He is a romantic and always looking for the ideal relationship. He wants a partner who will live up to his image of what a partner should be, treat him in the way he wants to be treated and love him in the way he wants to be loved. When, naturally, his partner fails to live up to this ideal, he is inclined to look around for someone who will.

At work he seeks an occupation that will enable him to withdraw inside himself and respond to his inner feelings. In advertising, he enjoys dreaming up ideas that will make his product attractive to others. As an author, he enjoys dreaming up the story and characters of his plot. As a poet or song writer, he enjoys dreaming of romantic interludes. As a sailor, he enjoys the outdoor nature of his life, the excitement of visiting new places and the possibility that one day he'll find his ideal environment. As an inventor, he dreams of being able to escape some of the drudgery of life and invents a machine or gadget that will enable him to do so. As a palm reader, astrologer or clairvoyant, he dreams of being able to foresee the future, and then avoid problems that will upset him, or of making everybody accept his vision of how the world really is. Whatever occupation a Lunarian does choose, his inner feelings are important to him and he wants a line of work that will satisfy them. The more restrictive his environment, the unhappier he is, and the more inclined he is to withdraw into the abstract world of his imagination away from the realities of life.

A subject's powers of rationalization (Head Line) must be carefully considered when dealing with the Lunarian type. Such is his predisposition to escape into the inner world of his imagination that if the clarity and consistency of these powers breaks down, his imagination will run away with him and he will, temporarily at least, have great difficulty in differentiating between his inner world and outside reality.

Overdeveloped

An overdeveloped mount is not a good sign to find because such persons will be so sensitive and so predisposed to escape into their imagination at the slightest provocation that they will be out of touch with reality. Many people dream great dreams, but they know they are dreaming. With an overdeveloped mount the slightest weakening in the powers of rationalization make it impossible for them to differentiate between a dream and reality. Insanity is the next stop and, because of their sensitivity, it might be virtually impossible for a psychiatrist to create an environment that would make them willing to come back into the real world.

Well balanced

Inner feelings and imagination are an essential part of human existence and on any hand a well-balanced development of this mount is important to find. Imagination makes communication possible. It also gives us the ability to hope and, as it allows us to visualize what things will be like when the bad times are over, it helps us persevere during times of difficulty. A good development of this mount shows the person has the imagination he needs, when he needs it.

Weak

A weak mount shows the person tends to lack inner feelings and consequently has no abstract world of his own. He is unable to escape from reality and has difficulty in dealing with anything of an abstract nature. He is ruled mostly by the here and now and dense materialism. He cannot understand the words of the civil rights activist who hopes for a better society, nor the warnings of the environmentalist who tries to show him that he is destroying his own world. Ideas and ideals leave him cold because he is unable to project his mind into the future and cannot understand how his actions of today will affect the lives of future generations.

Deficient

A deficient mount is a rarity but shows the person is extremely dense and totally unable to cope with anything that isn't in the immediate present. He cannot catch an idea, no matter how clearly it is presented, and, lacking any inner feelings of his own, he tends to be very insensitive.

▶ General Information

The mount is a mound and can be divided into physical, practical and mental worlds by noting whether it is most developed at its top, its centre or its base.

• If most developed in its upper part, the inner feelings will be elevated and seek fulfilment in some spiritual or intellectual way.
• If most developed in its centre, the inner feelings will seek fulfilment in the outside world.
• If the base is most developed, the inner feelings will seek fulfilment in some physical way.

'The Mount of Pluto'

Sometimes there is a knob of flesh low down on the mount close to the wrist. Some palmists call this the 'Mount of Pluto' and it has been referred to as the death instinct. This knob indicates that the person's inner feelings lie very deep and it is difficult for them to be fulfilled. Mysticism, witchcraft and various forms of magical ceremonies are often the only way the person can reach those feelings and find satisfaction.

Vertical lines

A single vertical line on this mount indicates the power of the inner feelings are increased and the imaginative abilities are used in a positive way. There are many books relating to the power of the mind and positive use of the imagination, claiming that if you visualize what you want, you will attract it to you. This is not unreasonable to a point. If a person constantly visualizes himself as a millionaire, he will gradually start to adopt courses of action that will take him closer to his desired goal. If he has the intelligence and willpower necessary to actualize his dream, there is no reason to suppose that he won't turn it into a reality. If, however, he doesn't have the necessary personal qualities to attain his goal, his visualizations are not likely to become a reality.

Crossbars

Crossbars show deep inner dissatisfactions and stress resulting from the negative use of the imagination. If this person is flying somewhere, he may visualize the plane crashing and killing all on board. If the crossbars are heavily marked he may visualize a more gruesome ending than just crashing into the ground. Benham has attributed a large number of health defects to marks found on this mount, but negative visualizations create stress, which in turn undermines the health of the individual.

Grill
A grill on this mount shows a conflict between positive and negative use of the imagination, and suggests a lot of stress. The person may imagine personal success, but also imagine hard times and the loss of everything he has worked to achieve.

Consistency

• Softer grades of hand consistency are common to the Lunarian type and show that although sensitive and a dreamer, the individual doesn't want to make the effort to turn those dreams into reality.
• Elastic consistency is much more positive because the person dreams his dreams and then makes an effort to turn them into reality. As a traveller, he will travel extensively and see much of the world. As an inventor, he will enjoy using his imagination to try to invent labour-saving devices for others as well as for himself.
• Hard consistency is unusual with this type, but I have seen it on sailors and people who are constantly on the move and live an outdoor life.

Colour

• White is a common colour to find on this type. Benham's description of the Lunarian type revolves around a person with white hands and very soft consistency. This combination shows a lazy, cold and selfish person who likes to spend his time dreaming and indulging his inner feelings.
• Pink shows a person willing to seek out the

company of others and find those who share similar
ideals.
• Red also shows warmth and suggests less sensitivity. Sometimes, as you look at the hand there is a red
patch which highlights the Mount of Luna. This
usually identifies Luna as the leading mount and
shows that the inner feelings are very strong and
intense.

Shape of the fingertips

• Spatulate tips add great originality to the imagination and often identify an inventor.
• Square tips show the imagination expresses itself
in a creative though practical way.
• Pointed or conic tips show the person is highly
unstable and constantly gets carried away by flights
of fancy. Some form of religious exaltation is
possible.
• Rounded tips are quite common and show a
balance between the practical and the idealistic. The
person's idealism is restrained or kept in check by
practical realities.

Length of the fingers

• Long fingers show the individual is extremely
sensitive, withdraws very much into himself and
always imagines personal slights where none are
intended.
• Short fingers incline a person to untidiness.

Fallacies
A number of fallacies have arisen over marks found
on the Mount. Many books say that crossbars show
journeys, while others say journeys are shown by
vertical lines. As a strong imagination inclines a

person to travel, vertical lines greatly increase this desire and if there are the means, the person will travel extensively. The crossbar fallacy has persisted because it is so difficult to define precisely what constitutes a journey, a point made even more complicated by the fact that many palmists say that travel means different things to different people. For example, a travel line on one person will mean a short trip to a neighbouring town whereas on another person the same line will mean a major intercontinental journey. Unfortunately, many palmists who by chance accurately relate a crossbar to a journey often overlook their many failures and put them down to difficulties in getting the timing right. Lines on any mount indicate the individual's psychological disposition, which may in turn result in certain actions. A desire to travel often results in a journey, but I have seen many so-called travel lines on people who have never travelled anywhere.

Another fallacy is that a circle on this mount shows death by drowning, and I have come across people who were very distressed by being told they were going to meet a watery end. Bearing in mind the ease with which palmists of the last century were able to examine the hands of those who had drowned, it is difficult to see how this idea arose in the first place. Cheiro claims to have spent a lot of time in mortuaries and, although it is possible that he saw this whorl on a number of people who had died by drowning, it would have been unreasonable for him to conclude that such a mark automatically showed the person would die through drowning. A circular whorl increases the power of this mount tremendously and as Lunarians are attracted to water, a Lunarian contemplating suicide would naturally be drawn to drowning as a way of escape.

THE MOUNT OF VENUS

*T*he Mount of Venus is found on the inside of the hand at the base of the thumb, but as it lies so close to Lower Mars its boundaries must be carefully observed. It is a difficult mount to classify and looking at a large number of hands is the only way to fix its appearance in your mind. On most hands it is generally the most prominent mount and this may make it difficult for you to gauge its relative degree of strength in your early endeavours.

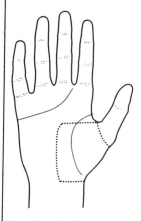

The Mount of Venus.

• If it is full and rounded, it is a strong mount, if not the dominant one. One or more vertical lines add great strength to the positive attributes of this mount and increase its power.

• This part of the hand is rarely hollow, but if it is flat, Venus is a weak or deficient mount. Crossbars or a grill show defects and weaken its positive characteristics.

Dominant

If Venus is the dominant mount on the hand, the person's active feelings are highly developed and, unlike a Lunarian, the last thing he wants to do is to withdraw inside himself. Authors refer to Venus as the mount of passion and Venusians, having strong active feelings, can't help being passionate people. They generally consider that feeling something, even if it is bad, is better than feeling nothing at all. They are bright, generous and agreeable and nothing would distress them more than the thought of others not liking their company.

To forgive and forget comes naturally to the Venusian type because any person harbouring a grudge against someone normally finds it difficult to forget their worries and enjoy himself. In fact, they can be too forgiving and too sympathetic for

their own good, finding it difficult if not impossible
to turn a deaf ear to a plea for help. This can sometimes be their undoing because it doesn't take long
for others to see the soft side of a Venusian's nature.
They are frequently imposed upon unnecessarily,
but such is their warmth they would rather be taken
advantage of several times than fail to help one
person who was genuinely in need

Of all the types, this is the most pleasant to meet.
A Venusian's greatest desire in life is to have fun and
be alive. Vibrant by nature, they go out of their way
to be pleasant to others and bring warmth and
brightness into other people's lives. They are
neither deep or profound, nor shrewd or clever, but
their warmth is genuine.

Venusians are greatly attracted to sex and sensual
pleasures, but they are not necessarily promiscuous
and many Venusians fight hard against their more
basic sexual desires. Although they love the warmth
of being close to another person and the ecstasy of
sharing intimate moments, a lasting relationship is
very important to them. For some Venusians there
are times when the temptations do get too much,
and in the heat of the moment they can get carried
away by their passions, but it is generally only a slip
and not a premeditated action. Once their passion
has cooled and they realize what they have done,
they often make an effort to ensure that it doesn't
happen again.

The Venusian's family is very important to him
and his home is usually tastefully decorated with
bright, but harmonious, colours. At work his warm
nature helps him succeed in occupations where he
can bring pleasure to others, or help them in some
way. Nursing and various forms of social work are
fields in which his sympathetic nature comes to the
fore and his warmth enables him to cheer everyone
else up. As his feelings respond so readily to
anything that appeals to his sense of beauty, he often
finds the worlds of art, music and fashion irresistible.

The Mount of Venus can vary from being a large unformed blob on the base of the hand to being a delicate, finely formed and well-proportioned mound. It is the formation of this mount that is your key to a full understanding of the way your subject's feelings are expressed. The finer the formation of the mount, the finer and more human the passions and feelings. The more this mount is like an unformed pad of flesh on the hand, the more basic are the passions and the more desires tend towards the sensual gratification of the senses.

Overdeveloped

An overdeveloped Venus is rare, but can be recognized because the mount is not well formed and appears to be just a very large blob of flesh at the base of the thumb. The excessive development shows that a person's base or physical world is dominant and indicates that he is dominated by feelings and passions. He burns with passion and tends to view others only from the standpoint of their ability to cater to his desires. According to Benham, an overdevelopment of this mount coupled with hard consistency and red colour is the sign of a ravisher, and in such a case the person's passions are so strong that once aroused, he becomes blinded by his desires and until they are satisfied nothing else will matter to him.

Well balanced

A good development of this mount is important to find on any hand. Active feelings drive us out of ourselves and towards other people. They enable us to enjoy life and be happy. If people didn't have active feelings, they would not be drawn towards each other and we would live in a cold and unfeeling world where everyone ignored everyone else.

Moreover, as sexual desire would be lacking, the human race would quickly cease to exist.

Weak
A weak Venus shows the person lacks active feelings and does not find himself driven towards others. They don't know what it's like to be filled with feelings of warmth and exuberance and because their need for others is not great, they are not driven to do things that will attract others to them. Consequently, they are prone to being unforgiving, intolerant and sometimes quite harsh in their treatment of others.

Deficient
A deficient Venus shows a person who doesn't need people and who can live with a minimal amount of human contact. Such people lack passion, see no reason as to why they should do things that would attract other people to them and will only be pleasant or warm towards others when they can help them further their aims. Their dominant mount will show what they enjoy doing, but they will be devoid of human feelings and once others get to know them, most people will find them unpleasant. Should they have Apollo as their dominant mount they will know how to make themselves agreeable, but their pleasantness will not be genuine and they will only seek to have others notice and admire them.

▶ General Information

The three worlds of the hand are important to note with this mount.

• If the mental world rules, art, music, fashion and

other intellectual ways of expressing passions and feelings will attract the individual.

• If the practical world is dominant, the individual's passions will express themselves in the outside world, and he will enjoy having a good time in the company of others, as well, perhaps, as caring for them or dealing with them in some way.

• A dominant physical world will show the individual's feelings seek an outlet in some physical way. Sex will always be very much on his mind.

The characteristics of this mount are generally considered to be very feminine, so a man with a developed, well-formed Venus will be feminine in his nature. This will be especially true if his fingers are on the long side, which shows that he thinks about what he feels.

Vertical lines

Vertical lines on this mount are often referred to as lines of influence, but lines of influence generally start on Lower Mars and run alongside the Life Line (see p. 170).

Vertical lines on the Mount of Venus actually show positive energy flows. Whatever the strength of the mount they are always good to find as they show positive feelings and a forgiving nature. They strengthen a weak mount and show that although the person may not always be driven to go out and enjoy himself, when he does, he knows how to have fun.

Crossbars

Crossbars are often found on this mount and show negative energy flows and a very strong desire for sex. If heavily marked, such persons' sexual desires are so strong that they may not be content to wait to find someone with whom they can establish a lasting relationship. The deeper these crossbars, the greater the sex drive and the more willing they are to overlook their sense of right and wrong in order to have them fulfilled. These crossbars also show they aren't always as forgiving as they could be. When offended, negative tendencies can lead them to become fixated on the offence and although they may not seek revenge, they will generally try to avoid the person who offended them.

Grill

A grill, when heavily marked, shows great excitability. Positive energy flows conflict with negative flows so although they are greatly attracted to others in a positive way, the negative flows take over and they spoil good non-sexual relationships by becoming sexually involved. They also fluctuate between holding grudges and then forgetting all about them.

Smooth mount

A smooth mount shows a great love of art, scenery, music, flowers and anything else that stimulates their feelings and appeals to their sense of beauty. It is not very common to find but I have seen it once on a singer of international renown.

Consistency

- Soft consistency inclines the person to be lazy and sensually indulgent.
- Elastic consistency shows a loving and sympathetic nature. If involved in the art world, the person will exert himself in his efforts either to produce works of beauty or, as is more common, help promote them.
- Hard consistency increases the person's sexual

passions and he will expend a great deal of energy in attempting to satisfy them, particularly if there are heavily marked crossbars on the mount.

Colour

● Pink is the normal colour to find on a Venusian type.
● Red means there is too much warmth and intensity in the person.
● White cools the individual tremendously. I have heard many white-handed Venusians say that they are unable to feel as much as they would like to feel.

Flexibility

● Flexible thumbs are common with this type because such is their desire to enjoy themselves and associate with others, they are more willing to adapt to the ways of those they meet. Also, as they have such strong sexual desires, accepting a lover who is not quite what they want is often better than having no lover at all.
● A stiff thumb shows persons who are more morally upright and more willing to subdue their passions until they find the right person. They may have to wait a long time and no one will know of the inner desires they have to struggle against.

Thumb

A small thumb indicates a person who is unable to control their passions and if there are crossbars or a grill, they are likely to be very promiscuous. Even if they would prefer to be more morally upright, they will, in the heat and passion of the moment, be unable to control their desires.

Skin texture
Regardless of whether the skin texture is coarse or
fine, Venusians are always warm, generous and
sympathetic. However, with coarse texture they
will be more down to earth and basic in their sexual
instincts, and they may also tend to be on the crude
side.

ACTIVE AND PASSIVE ZONES OF THE HAND

*T*he hand can be divided into active and passive zones by drawing a line from the centre of the Mount of Saturn down to the wrist. This theory has been put forward by leading palmists such as Arnold Holtzmann (see p. 207). Once you understand the significance of each mount, it becomes easy to see the logic behind the active/passive theory.

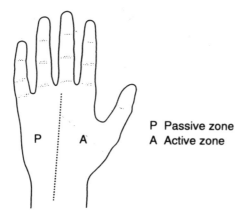

P Passive zone
A Active zone

- If the hand is more developed on the thumb side of this line, the person is active and seeks to impress himself on his environment.
- If the hand is more developed on the percussion side of the line, the person is passive and allows his environment to impress itself upon him.

- Jupiter, Lower Mars and Venus lie in the active zone.
- Saturn is in the centre and doesn't count.
- Apollo, Mercury, Upper Mars and Luna lie in the passive zone.

Active

- Jupiter is active because it indicates the person's desire to dominate, control, direct or command others.
- Lower Mars is active because it indicates the person's desire to push and force a way forward in life.
- Venus is active because it indicates the person's desire to enjoy himself and to brighten up everything around him.

Passive

- Apollo is passive because it indicates the person's desire to express himself and be noticed or admired by others.
- Mercury indicates a person's desire to communicate and is also considered to be passive. A Mercurian surgeon adjusts his operating procedures to suit the complexities of the body he is operating on.
- Upper Mars is passive because it only springs into action when it has to resist pressures brought to bear by outside influences.
- Luna is passive because the inner feelings respond to the environment and only withdraw from it during times of difficulty or unpleasantness.

The fingers

The way the hand is held indicates the present

psychological disposition of your subject and is important to note when considering the longitudinal division of the hand. The fingers can lean towards the active side of the hand, appear straight, or lean towards the passive side.

Leaning towards active

When the fingers lean towards the active side of the hand and the active mounts are prominent, the person is very keen to impress himself on his environment and make things happen. If the active mounts are not prominent, it shows that the person currently has some reason for trying to impress himself on his environment and cause things to happen.

Straight

Straight fingers are normal and although there isn't much a palmist can say about them in a reading, they are always good to find.

Leaning towards passive

If the fingers lean towards the passive side of the hand and the active mounts are prominent, there is some reason why, even though not normally inclined to passivity, the person is refraining from impressing himself on his environment. This may be due to some aspect of his current situation. If the active mounts are low on the list of prominence, the person is particularly passive in his attitude and rarely does anything to impress himself upon his environment or make things happen.

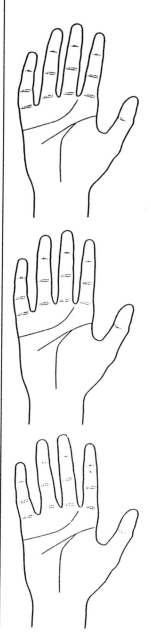

READING A
DIFFICULT HAND

When the hand is unbalanced and there are clear differences in the relative strengths of each mount it is easy to read from mount types. However, on a well-balanced hand it can be difficult to select the dominant mount and place the others in their order of prominence. When faced with this hand, it is often easier to use a process of elimination. Determining which mounts are not prominent can simplify matters enormously. But although using a system of elimination can be of great help, it does not always enable you to determine the most dominant mount. There will be times when you find yourself unable to make a final decision and in such situations, if you can find no further clues to help you, asking your subject for help is the only way of settling the matter.

Tell your subject the difficulties, explain the characteristics of each mount and then ask him to tell you which of his desires are strongest. If he is unable to help, try offering an option between two different lifestyles. For instance, if you were unable to decide whether Saturn or Venus was the dominant mount, you might ask him to imagine that he had reached a crossroads in life and was forced to choose between lifestyle A and lifestyle B.

Lifestyle A (Saturn) would be very stable and financially secure. He would have unlimited opportunities to probe deeply into things and find answers to any questions that bothered him. Others would respect his opinions, seeking his advice, and would be unable to take advantage of him. However, on the down side, he would be required to spend a great deal of time away from his family and friends. Although he would have people with whom to discuss things, his sex life would be minimal and his social life would be dull and uninteresting.

Lifestyle B (Venus) would be the complete opposite. He would be a very happy person, have an excellent sex and social life, and also spend a lot of time with his family and those he loved. Beauty would surround him and he'd find it very easy to get on with almost everyone he met. However, other people would tend to see him as quite superficial and refuse to take his opinions seriously. They would find it easy to take advantage of him and as a result his financial affairs would be uncertain and go through great ups and downs.

When presented with these options, a Saturnian would be inclined to choose lifestyle A whereas a Venusian would be inclined to choose lifestyle B.

PALMISTRY ASSESSMENT FORM
(PHYSICAL ASPECTS OF THE HAND)

*P*almistry is a complex science and it is very easy for a palmist to overlook one or two small points and make a large number of highly inaccurate statements. To avoid making mistakes you must make the effort to note each point of the hand before you say anything. Once each aspect of the hand has been observed, you can then select a starting point from which to begin your reading. At the end of this section there is an assessment form for the physical aspects of the hand and the points on this list should be checked off at the start of any reading. It is only a check list and although it may appear laborious and time consuming, it will make sure nothing is overlooked and so reduce the possibility of errors.

Once you have checked off the points on the assessment form your next problem is to choose a point from which to begin your reading. As a beginner you might find it advantageous to use the assessment form as a guide and start talking about the skin texture, then deal with the consistency of the hand and then its flexibility. As you progress through each point you will begin to build a picture of your subject and relate the point you are dealing with to the ones that have gone before. Each reader has his own ideas about how a palm should be read and after you have had some experience you can adjust the system to suit yourself.

To be completed for both left and right hands

 1 Left or right handed   _____

 2 Skin texture   _____

 3 Consistency   _____

 4 Flexibility   _____

 5 Palm colour   _____

 6 Nails   _____

 7 Hand as a whole   _____

 8 Finger lengths   _____

 9 Smooth or knotty fingers   _____

10 Finger phalanges   _____

11 Finger shapes   _____

12 Palm shape   _____

13 Finger spacings   _____

14 Size of the thumb   _____

15 Top phalange   _____

16 Second phalange   _____

17 Base phalange   _____

18 Flexibility of top joint   _____

19 Flexibility of bottom joint   _____

20 Thumb stance   _____

21 Dominant mount   _____

22 Secondary mount   _____

23 Third mount   _____

24 Fourth mount   _____

25 Fifth mount   _____

26 Sixth mount   _____

27 Seventh mount   _____

28 Overdeveloped mount?   _____

29 Deficient mount?   _____

30 Markings on Jupiter   _____

31 Markings on Saturn   _____

32 Markings on Apollo   _____

33 Markings on Mercury   _____

34 Markings on Lower Mars   _____

35 Markings on Upper Mars   _____

36 Markings on Luna   _____

37 Markings on Venus   _____

38 Plain of Mars   _____

39 Active and passive zones   _____

40 Active and passive finger   _____
   stance

This list is fairly simple and straightforward, but as you gain experience you can develop your own list and add points to it.

PART II

CHIROMANCY

THE LINES OF
THE HAND

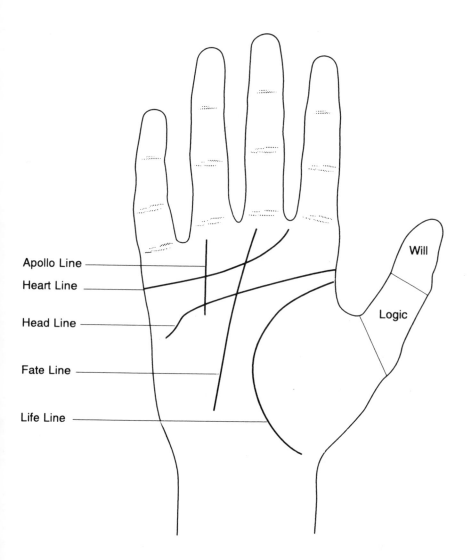

Apollo Line

Heart Line

Head Line

Fate Line

Life Line

Will

Logic

*M*any contemporary authors base their entire system of reading palms on the lines of the hand. They encourage their students to try and classify the hand into one of four types (Earth, Fire, Water and Air) depending on the linear patterns of the palm. Unfortunately, although a large number of hands do fall into one of these categories, a great many don't, and this means that any reader using this system is constantly confronted with hands he or she simply cannot read. In palmistry, as in other scientific fields, if a theory does not fit every known possibility, it is most unwise to persist with it.

In the traditional system of reading hands the lines add colour to the picture already drawn by the physical aspects of the hand. They tell a great deal about the psychological idiosyncrasies of an individual and the details of his life, though it is important to remember that they indicate the details of an individual's life as seen from a personal point of view and not somebody else's. (People may be successful in the eyes of the world but that does not necessarily mean that they have found the kind of success they really seek and consequently lines of success may be poorly marked on their hand.) Too many students are excited by the possibility of predicting future events and begin by trying to read a palm from the lines. But as lines must be read in conjunction with the physical aspects of the hand, this tendency normally leads to a high degree of error, and many sincere students give up their endeavours in despair.

Reading from lines is the most delicate part of palmistry and great care must be taken as it is all too easy to make a mistake. You should always make a point of staying within the limitations of your knowledge because once a statement has been made, it can be very difficult to retract. In your early attempts you should content yourself with picking out the main lines and telling your subject what these indicate. Then, as you become more familiar with these lines and have had some practice in interpreting them, you can start broadening the scope of your readings and incorporating the minor lines.

The Heart, Head and Life Lines are good lines to start on because they appear on almost every hand, though their starting points, their course through the hand, and their ending points vary considerably. The Fate Line also appears on most hands so it too can be considered to be a main line. Other lines, however, are often absent and should be viewed as minor lines.

After having studied the physical aspects of the hand, the first step when dealing with the lines is to look at the main lines and see if it is possible to pick the dominant one. One line is often (though not always) stronger or more prominent than the others, and this will tell you a lot about your subject.

• No matter what desires are indicated by the mounts, if the Heart Line is the most dominant line your subject's life will always be regulated by their affections.
• A dominant Head Line (powers of rationalization) will show that much of a person's life is regulated by their mind or what they think.
• A dominant Life Line will show a person's life is governed by matters concerning their physical and personal self.
• Should the Fate Line be dominant then work, security and stability will govern much of a person's life.

Each line should be examined individually and careful attention must be paid to its character. Ideally, the line should be clear and even from start to finish, but this is rarely the case and observing the changes in character in a line's course through the hand tells you about the changing conditions of your subject's life.

● If well marked, clear and even, the aspects of life indicated by the line can be expected to be running smoothly.
● If broad and shallow, chained or islanded, then periods of difficulty can be expected.

Strangely enough, most predictive work is done from an analysis of the character of a line rather than from any of the special signs and marks many books tell their students to be on the look out for.

THE HEART LINE

*A*n analysis of the Heart Line will enable you to determine the depth and quality of a person's emotional nature. The longer and clearer this line, the more a person is governed by love and affection for family, friends, relatives and mankind in general. The shorter the line, the less influenced a person is by such matters and the less inclined to care for others or pay attention to the desires and emotional needs of family and friends.

Love is such a powerful force in human nature that many people consult a palm reader with the specific intention of finding out about their love life. They want to know when they are going to get married or find a rewarding and long-lasting relationship. Unfortunately, as palmistry deals with the overall course of a person's life, this isn't always easy. In most cases all a palmist can do is note the nature and quality of the line and restrict himself to talking about his client's emotional disposition and the good or bad periods he is likely to go through.

▶ The Length of the Line

Very long
A line that stretches all the way across the hand is an extremely long line and shows an excessively developed emotional nature. Persons with this line are completely governed by love and affection for others. They view love as an ideal and are unable to understand that too much love can be as bad as not enough. They are very possessive, so much so that they will be hurt and jealous if their loved one even looks at another person. They consequently suffer a great deal in love, especially since people with a more balanced disposition find them oppressive and try

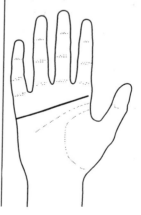

not to get too involved. I have often seen this line on religious and political fanatics.

Beginning on Jupiter

When the line starts on the centre of Jupiter it is also a long line and although not excessively developed, such subjects are still influenced by love. They are affectionate and give a lot to those they care for. However, they expect a lot in return and are easily hurt when their giving goes unappreciated. With any overdevelopment of this line it is important to remember that there are very few people who can give without any thought of receiving in return. The more people give, the easier it is for them to be hurt or disappointed when there is no suitable recompense for their efforts.

Beginning on Jupiter and Saturn

A line starting between the fingers of Jupiter and Saturn shows a more balanced emotional disposition. Although the subject is capable of loving deeply, they are not dominated by their emotions and are realistic enough to realize that there has to be plenty of give and take in a successful relationship.

Beginning on Saturn

A line starting on Saturn is a short line and shows that love and affection are not important aspects of life. Although there is a capacity for love and they need a mate, they tend to be more concerned with personal desires. Many authors have referred to this as a sensual Heart Line, but as they are not motivated by powerful feelings of love, their attraction to another stems from sexual desire and the need for companionship. They like rather than love, and any giving is motivated by what is

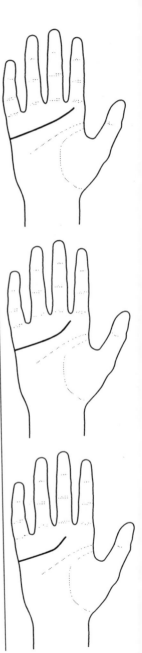

expected or by what is necessary to maintain a relationship and keep their partner happy.

Beginning on Apollo

A line that starts on the Mount of Apollo is a very short line and shows people who are cold in their emotions and have little feeling for others. In relationships they are selfish and inclined to use others to serve their own purposes. They give because they want something in return and never to make others happy.

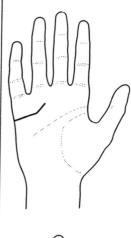

▶ The Curve or Sweep of the Line

An upward curve

The commencement of the line tells a great deal about a person's emotional attitude. If it sweeps upwards it shows an extroverted emotional disposition. The curve itself increases the length of the line and the consequent strength of the affections, but the upward sweep shows a receptive, outgoing emotional nature. It is generally accepted by most contemporary authors that this upward sweep shows a person who is very sexual in his relationships. But before committing yourself to any statements on this point it is important to remember that although the subject's positive emotional disposition will incline him to want to be physically close to the person he loves, the actual degree of sexual activity will depend very much on the development of Venus and the condition of the Life Line. It is also generally accepted that when let down in a relationship, although a person with this upward sweep can be shattered and distraught for a time, he gets over his disappointments relatively quickly, preferring to leave the past in the past, and willingly responding to new emotional possibilities.

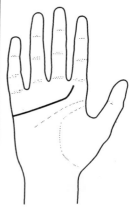

A downward curve

A line that sweeps downwards at its commencement shows an emotionally introverted nature. As
the Heart Line dips towards the Head Line it indicates a conflict between what people think and what
they feel for other people. They place mental
restrictions on their emotions and don't allow themselves to feel for others or interact with them
emotionally until they have rationalized their feelings. This control unfortunately only creates a
sense of emotional emptiness, which, over a period
of time, develops into an emotional need. When
they meet someone who fulfils their mental concept
of what they are looking for, all their pent-up
emotional energies are released, the heart runs away
with the head and they become so blinded by love
that they are unable to think rationally. Once they
have let go, should this relationship break down,
they will have the greatest difficulty getting over
their loss, especially as they won't allow themselves
to fall in love again until they meet another person
who satisfies their mental requirements. In fact,
should Luna or Saturn be dominant mounts,
recovery may take many years.

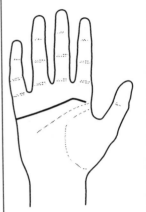

From a physical point of view, emotionally introverted subjects are less sexual in their relationships
because their introverted nature makes them a
seeker of something more than just sex and companionship. They seek someone who will provide the
love that they crave and, as what they think is
constantly interfering with how they feel, they are
unable to relax and enjoy a good, personally
rewarding, long-term sexual relationship.

There are reasons as to why mentality interferes
with the natural flow of emotional energies. Cheiro
has said that the drooping Heart Line is a sure sign
of unhappiness in early life and if this indication is
found in both hands, the probabilities of an
unhappy childhood are high. But since the concept
of an unhappy childhood is relative to experience, if

they never experienced periods of real happiness in life, it can often be difficult for them to accept that their childhood wasn't happy. When dealing with this aspect of palmistry in a reading, I generally prefer to tell my clients that their childhood wasn't as emotionally fulfilling as it could have been and that they may also have had difficulty interacting with their family in an emotional way. Even if a person with this indication was well cared for, such is the fragility of a child's emotional nature that an almost unnoticeable incident to an adult could be very disturbing to a three-year-old, who only has three years of stored data against which to rationalize the event. In such a case, the child would develop an emotional need, which, if it wasn't catered to by the parents, would cause withdrawal and the development of a mental control over emotional response.

If this downward sweep is found only in the right or active hand then it is often the result of subjects losing their family support system and having no one upon whom to call in times of need. This absence of a support system would then cause them to seek a relationship that would enable them to establish some solid emotional foundations. In one case, the subject chose a career that went against his parents wishes and, although they accepted his decision, they refused to support him in it. Not having anyone else to turn to, he became emotionally introverted and, in his love life, he ceased looking for just a companion and began to seek someone who could give him the love and emotional support he needed to continue pursuing his goals. In other words, his mind started to interfere with the natural flow of his emotional energies because he knew, subconsciously at least, what he wanted from a relationship. When he met potential mates, whether or not he pursued the possibility of a lasting relationship depended very much on their ability to cater to his introverted emotional needs.

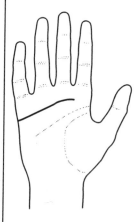

The greater the downward sweep of this line the greater the emotional need of the subject. If the line only dips slightly then the person is only slightly inclined to be introverted in his emotional nature.

A drooping line

In an extreme situation the Heart Line droops right down into the mount of Lower Mars and in such a case the emotions are very strong but also tightly restricted by the mentality. With the Heart Line's source in Lower Mars, such is the power of the affections that when such people do find what they think they are looking for, their emotions run away with them, any previous plans or intentions are completely forgotten, and they become unable to behave rationally. With this line you must also be on your guard for crossbars or negative energy flows because feelings of hate can often be as powerful and overwhelming as feelings of love.

A straight line

A straight Heart Line shows a balance between the extroverted and the introverted. However, this is rare as on most hands there is almost always a slight curve to the line. If it doesn't incline up or down then there is usually a branch line which will indicate the direction of the subject's emotional inclinations.

▶ General Information

Character of the line

The character or quality of the line can tell you about your subject's emotions and the consequent quality of his emotional life. Bear in mind that it's unusual to see a Heart Line of consistent quality

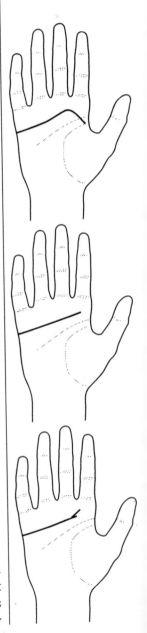

and you will normally see a series of changes which will show the changing nature of your subject's emotional life.

- A line that is clear, deep, and even from start to finish shows an emotional consistency and indicates the person will have a rewarding emotional life.
- A broad and shallow line shows the love nature is shallow and insincere and that emotional life will never be meaningful nor rewarding.
- A line that is thin in proportion to the other lines on the hand shows an emotionally self-centred person.
- If the line is long, the person will see himself as loving, but, like a person with a broad and shallow line, out-of-sight will be out-of-mind.
- An island shows a period of instability, unsettledness and emotional difficulty.
- A series or chain of islands shows extended periods of unsettledness and emotional difficulty.
- A break in the line shows a complete change in the emotional life of the subject – often brought about by a person being badly let down by a loved one.
- A dot or hollow in the line is the most serious of all, and indicates a period of severe emotional difficulty.

The quality of the line after a break, island, or dot should always be carefully noted as it will often indicate how well the subject recovers from a difficulty. It is quite normal to see a defect followed by a very thin line showing the difficulty has caused withdrawal. Cheiro said that when the line is very thin at the percussion the subject will end his life as a lonely and friendless person. But many people become emotionally self-centred, demanding, and difficult to cope with in their later years, and whether or not they are lonely and friendless is likely to depend very much on their family and the quality of the geriatric care they receive.

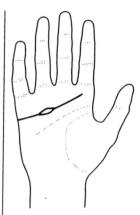

An island

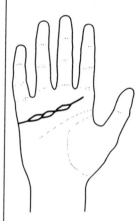

A chain of islands

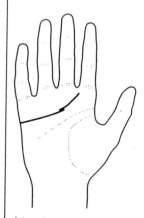

A break

Extra lines

● Little lines that rise into the Heart Line are positive indications and show affections or friendships which increase the quality of a person's emotional existence.

● Split lines that fall away from the Heart Line are negative indications and show emotional depressions. Some friend, loved one, or family member is detracting from the quality of the subject's emotional life and causing a drain on his emotional system. When this split line is seen the emotional drain lasts for as long as it continues to run underneath the Heart Line.

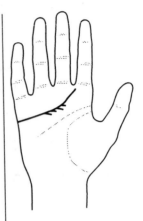

Lines rising

Colour

● A red line increases the intensity of the emotional nature and consequently the relative strength of the line.

● Pink is always good to find as the subject will be warm and genial in his treatment of friends and those he cares for.

● White shows coldness and even if the line is very long, the subject will be self-contained and undemonstrative in regard to love.

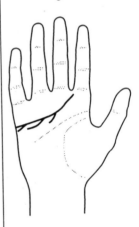

Split lines falling away

▶ Timing of Events

The dating of events on the Heart Line is extremely difficult and as there is so much disagreement between palmists as to where this line actually starts, many students never even try to time an event. Modern palmists claim the Heart Line begins on the percussion and some say that because the line is usually consistent on this side of the hand, they have chosen this starting point for reasons of simplicity and coherence. Traditionalists say the line starts on the Mount of Jupiter and are more willing to accept the difficulties involved when using this starting point. The nature of the line under Jupiter can vary dramatically from hand to hand, but bearing in mind the ease with which events can cause lasting alterations to a child's whole emotional attitude, Jupiter is the most logical starting point for this line.

It is only possible to date events on lines that are fairly clear and consistent. But by measuring the line and then dividing its length by seventy (to get the amount of space occupied by one year) one can achieve modestly satisfying results, particularly in regards to past events. I set a small pair of dividers to a spacing of one centimetre and then measure the line from start to finish. Once I know its length I can then set the dividers to ten-year intervals (normally 0.9 to 1.2 centimetres) and work my way through the line using judgment to gauge the exact year of any marks or changes to the character of the line. Unlike most authors, I do not support the idea that a year in youth takes more space on a line than a year in middle or old age. Time is a consistent factor, each day has twenty-four hours and it seems reasonable to assume that each year takes up an equal amount of space on the line, regardless of the person's age. However, as the emotional nature of most people is very complex and the measurements involved so fine, a detailed analysis of past or future events is extremely difficult and only major marks can be taken into consideration. Consequently, should you decide to experiment with this system, great care will have to be taken when trying to predict future events.

▶ Active and Passive Hands

Checking the line in both hands can tell you a great deal about how experience has altered the emotional disposition of your subject. If the Heart Line is longer and better marked on the right or active hand you will know that over the years the person has become more affectionate and loving. Unfortunately, it is generally more common to see this line better marked in the left or passive hand indicating that experience has caused the very opposite.

THE HEAD LINE

Whereas the Heart Line indicates emotional energies, the Head Line indicates mental energies and powers of rationalization, the scope of mentality, how people think and the type of decisions they make. It has traditionally been accepted that the Head Line shows a person's degree of intelligence, but nothing could be further from the truth. Although long, clear and well-formed Head Lines are often seen on the hands of very intelligent people, they are also seen on the hands of dull and unintelligent ones. A person's degree of intelligence is indicated by the physical aspects of his hand, particularly the second phalanx of the thumb. The Head Line only indicates a person's ability to put intelligence to use by responding to what he thinks, making plans and following them through.

▶ The Length of the Line

The subject's degree of intelligence is not necessarily relative to the length of the head line. For example, some unintelligent people may have excessively long lines. It is therefore important to note the overall character of the hand before trying to gauge intelligence.

Very long
An excessively long line stretches all the way across the hand and shows people who are governed by their mentality. They rationalize everything and subject all aspects of their life to scrutiny. As the mind has so much control, even the affections are allowed only to operate within the limitations dictated by the mentality. Unfortunately, this

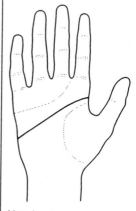

Very long

means that they limit their life to matters that their mind can deal with and anything that is beyond the scope of their understanding is blocked out or ignored. This is a calculating nature, but because they are so 'locked in' to what they think, when forced into any situation that is too much for their mentality to deal with, they cannot cope, and if there is no escape, they break down.

Long

A long line shows many of the same characteristics as an excessive line. However, although such people are calculating and subject almost all aspects of their life to what they think, they are not quite so limited by mentality. They make good use of their mentality, but are inclined to be rational in their plans and approach to life.

Medium

A medium line shows the powers of rationalization are adequately developed. They make good use of their mentality, but are not limited by a need to be rational or far-sighted in everything they do, plan or hope for.

Short

Whereas a long line shows the person's mentality has too much influence over his life, a short line indicates it does not have enough. The person's mind lacks the capacity to make full use of the available intelligence, and he is short-sighted in his decisions, thinking in terms of the immediate future.

Very short

A very short line indicates a very limited mentality. No matter how much intelligence is indicated

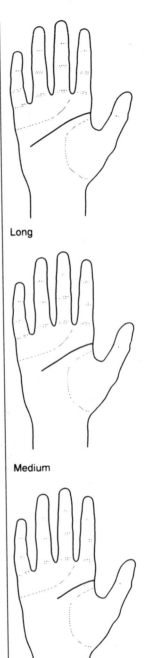

Long

Medium

Short

by other aspects of the hand, little or no use is made of it. Such subjects' powers of rationalization operate in a limited sphere, they rarely make long-term decisions, and even if they do they generally forget them. Because their mind operates in a very limited way, they have a one-track mind and, if inherently intelligent, may know a great deal about one subject but virtually nothing about anything else.

▶ **The Starting Point of the Line**

Wide separation from Life Line
When the Head Line starts high on the Mount of Jupiter and is widely separated from the Life Line, it indicates that pride greatly influences the way in which the person thinks. Almost all his decisions are based on the assumption that he is right, although the opposite is the case. It has always been accepted that this indication shows a person who is very rash in the decisions he makes, but Holtzman (see p. 207) was one of the first authors to define clearly why such a person is foolhardy in his decision making processes.

Narrow separation from Life Line
At its commencement, the narrower the space between the Head and Life Lines, the more the mentality is influenced by matters concerning physical and personal self. A small space is good to find as it indicates that although personal matters influence any decisions the person makes, they do not restrict him. The subject is mentally confident, but not overly so.

Initial link with Life Line
When the Head Line touches the Life Line at its

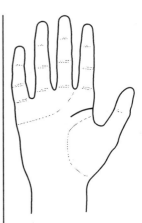
Very short

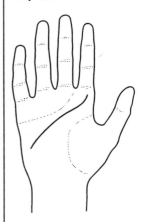
Wide separation

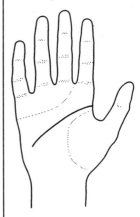
Narrow separation

commencement mental caution is indicated as matters of physical and personal self will actually restrict or inhibit any decisions the person makes.

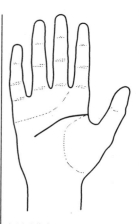

Initial link

Close association with Life Line

In an extreme situation the Head and Life Lines are closely joined for a considerable distance and reach well into the palm before separating. This shows a person who is very sensitive and whose mentality is greatly inhibited by matters concerning his personal and physical self. He has difficulty being decisive and is always anxious about the consequences of any decision he does make. He is consequently mentally unadventurous, very cautious and unwilling to take chances with anything that affects him personally. It is probable that during his childhood he was not encouraged to think for himself or make his own decisions, and he may even have been oppressed or prevented from doing so. The point at which the two lines separate shows the point at which he started to break free of this. If Saturn is prominent, he will miss many opportunities through being hesitant and by his need to be sure everything will work out successfully before he commits himself to anything. If the finger of Jupiter is weak, then feelings of inferiority and personal worthlessness are almost certain. (A weak Jupiter, drooping Heart Line and closely joined Head and Life Lines are an almost certain sign of someone who had a very unhappy childhood. Such people are often charming, intelligent and easy to get along with, but their manner of self-expression is often a facade and they break down easily when under pressure.)

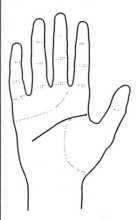

Close association

Commencement at Lower Mars

A line that starts inside the Life line on Lower Mars shows your subject is extremely sensitive and so touchy about anything that affects him personally that he is argumentative and in constant conflict with other people. He is always on the defensive and very changeable and erratic because although he makes each decision with great force and resolve, such is the intensity of his mind that each decision is an independent event and often fails to take account of the ones that have preceded it. (On a white hand this indication is not quite so serious because the coldness of the person's nature will greatly reduce the intensity and changeability of the mentality.)

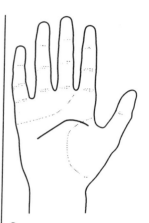

Commencement Lower Mars

Commencement within the hand

A line that doesn't start until some way into the hand shows a person who didn't start to think for himself until later in life. The point at which the line starts shows the age at which he started to think for himself and live according to the dictates of his own mind.

Commencement high on Jupiter

Very occasionally you will see a line that starts high on the Mount of Jupiter and sweeps down and touches the Life Line before stretching out across the hand. In such a case the person is mentally ambitious, always seeking to improve his status and have complete control over his life. However, because the line touches the Life Line, the ambitious nature of the mentality is tinged with caution and this prevents him from becoming too ambitious and overreaching himself. I have seen this line on a number of people who started with nothing and raised themselves to very affluent lifestyles.

Commencement within hand

▶ The Sweep of the Line

A Head Line can be straight, sweep down into Luna or curve up towards Mercury. A downward sweep

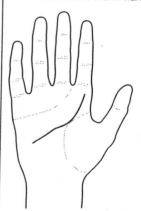

Commencement high on Jupiter

to the line is most common, straight is frequent, but an upward curve is quite rare and shows unusual mental characteristics.

Straight
A straight line shows a level-headed, practical mentality and someone who rationalizes everything according to the realities of their external environment. Such people are materialistic and very realistic.

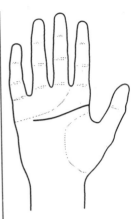

Straight

A downward curve
A downward curve to the line shows that inner feelings and imagination strongly influence the thought patterns and type of decisions the person makes. The greater the downward curve, the greater the inclination to be idealistic, overlook the realities of the external world and make decisions that are based on inner feelings, ideas, and ideals.

A slight curve
A slight curve to the line shows someone who thinks in a practical and realistic way, but who, unlike a person with a completely straight line, is not limited by the realities of his immediate environment and can, when the situation demands, respond to abstract ideas and ideals.

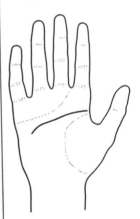

Downward curve

A slope
A noticeable slope to the line shows someone who is idealistic, imaginative and creative. A very sloping Head Line shows the mentality is greatly influenced by the imagination. This line increases the relative strength of Luna and the person is consequently very sensitive and idealistic and inclined to be something of a daydreamer. Many authors have suggested that this very sloping line

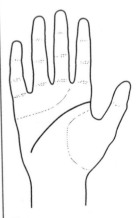

Slope

shows an inclination towards depression, but depression is sometimes the result of unrealistic expectations in life and anyone with this type of Head Line, being so influenced by the abstract world of his imagination, would be prone to being unrealistic in his expectations. (This type of line coupled with a great many cross lines on the hand and fingers is often seen on people who suffer from chronic depression.)

Extreme slope

An extremely sloping line shows an immensely sensitive individual. The Head Line appears to cling to the Life Line and this indicates that matters of personal and physical self (Life Line) greatly restrict the natural flow of the mental energies. As the mind is so strongly influenced by the imagination, the person is very unrealistic in his expectations and the consequent disappointments cause deep depressions.

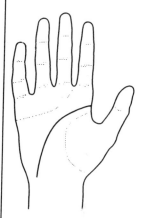

Extreme slope

Dropping into Luna

When you see a sloping Head Line you must increase your estimate of its length. But although a Head Line that clings to the Life line and drops straight into Luna is a long line showing mental ability, in terms of mental control it can only be considered to be a short line because it only crosses a short distance into the hand.

Upward curve at end

A line that has an upward curve at its end has been called the 'croupier's rake' and indicates a calculating, materialistic and acquisitive mentality. As the line curves upwards and away from the Mount of Luna, ideas, ideals and inner feelings have very little influence on the way the individual thinks or the

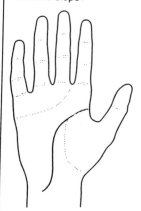

Dropping into Luna

decisions he makes. A sloping line allows a person to be understanding because when he sees someone in difficulty or distress he can visualize himself in the same situation. But an upward sweep to the line shows the mental patterns are unimaginative and the calculating nature of the individual inclines him to see those over whom he has authority as machines rather than people. He can, as a consequence, be extremely demanding and very unsympathetic towards those who don't live up to his expectations. However, because the line sweeps up towards Mercury, a subject with this line can often be too clever and efficient for his own good.

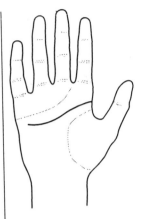

Upward curve

▶ The Ending of the Line

The quality of the line at its end will tell you about the person's mental capabilities during the later stages of life.

● If the end is clear and well marked, the mental faculties will continue to function normally.
● If it loses its clarity and begins to weaken or fade, the mental powers will weaken and begin to fade.
● If the line fragments and looks like a tassel that seems to merge into the capillary lines of the palm, the subject will become forgetful, erratic and probably senile.

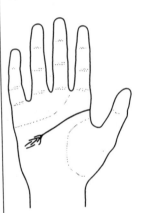

Tasseled line

● A fork at the end of the line is a good sign and shows a person who is mentally versatile. If one prong is straight and the other drops into Luna, he is able to rationalize things from either a practical or imaginative point of view. Sometimes he will be very level-headed and realistic while at other times he will be idealistic and imaginative. The type of decisions he normally makes and what he will be inclined to do when under pressure can be determined by noting which of the two branch lines is stronger.

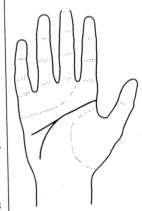

Forked line

• A triple-pronged fork is occasionally seen and shows a very versatile mind. Normally, one branch runs up towards Mercury, another is straight, and the third drops down into Luna. It shows a person who can be calculating and efficient, practical and realistic, or imaginative and idealistic. The strongest line will show the point of view from which he normally rationalizes his decisions and the others will show the different perspectives from which he can view an issue. For instance, if the line that curves into Luna is the strongest then although he may talk about doing things in a cold, calculating and efficient way (upward branch), when it comes to actually doing them, the imaginative and idealistic side of his nature will prevent him from following through and doing the things he said he would do. But his ability to view things from differing perspectives enables him to surprise others with his conversation because one minute he is talking about the ideal situation, the next he is talking in terms of practical reality and immediately afterwards he is explaining to people that if a particular objective is to be achieved then a certain course of action must be adopted without regard to the needs or desires of those who would have to suffer. As a lawyer he can be unbeatable because he can always find an angle or perspective from which to argue his case, and make even the most dreadful of crimes seem quite excusable.

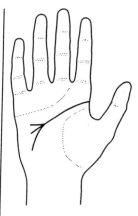

Triple fork

▶ General Information

Character of the line
As with other lines the character of the Head Line frequently changes as it proceeds through the hand and each change reflects a change to the thinking processes of the individual, the age at which it occurs and the length of time it lasts.

● A line that is clear, even and well defined
throughout its length is always good to see as it
shows clarity of thought, continuity of purpose,
good memory and an ability to exercise self-control.
● A broad and shallow line shows mental inertia
and a person who allows himself to drift through
life without any clear or well-defined idea of where
he is going.
● A thin line shows a person unable to withstand
much in the way of mental stress or pressure.
● An island shows a period of mental instability.
The person is unable to collect his thoughts and is
very inconsistent in his decisions. His powers of
rationalization will not function properly during
this period and he is likely to make a number of bad
or unwise decisions.
● A chain shows an extended period of time when
the mentality is divided, unsettled and simply not
functioning properly. Any person with a chained
Head Line should be encouraged to avoid intellectual pursuits and any situation in which he is likely
to experience mental stress.
● If you see dots on the line it shows severe mental
disturbances at the time they appear.
● Very occasionally you will see a section of the
line that is much deeper than normal and this
indicates a period of severe mental stress.

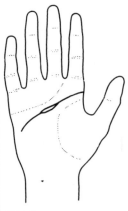

Island

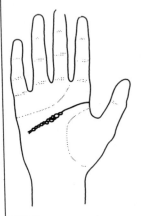

Chain

When you see defects on the Head Line you must
make a careful note as to the relative strength of the
Mount of Luna as defects on this line are much
more serious when Luna is strongly developed. You
must also note the condition of the line after the
defect as this will tell you whether or not the person
recovers completely.

Change of direction
Sometimes the Head Line appears to change its
direction and this shows that at the time of the

change the person changes the way he thinks and the criteria upon which he bases his decisions.

• A line that begins with a gentle curve and suddenly rises slightly and runs straight across the hand shows that at the point where the line changes course the person began to be more practical, realistic and materialistic in his decisions.

• Sometimes a straight line changes direction and curves sharply down into Luna and this indicates that in the early part of his life the person was practical and realistic, but later changed his mental attitude, allowed himself to be influenced by his imagination and began to follow his dreams. Any change to the direction of this line must be carefully noted as it shows a change in the way the individual thinks and rationalizes his actions.

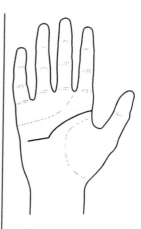

Gentle curve, sudden rise

Extra lines

• An incidental line that starts on Jupiter and joins the Head Line some way down the hand shows that at the time of the join the person began to become very mentally ambitious.

• Split lines that leave the Head line and run in an upward direction show periods when the person tries to develop a greater mental control over his life.

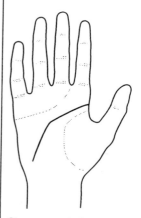

Sharp curve to Luna

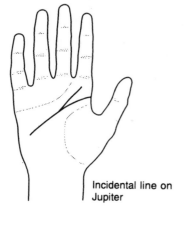

Incidental line on Jupiter

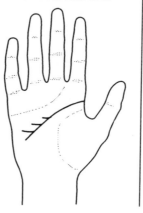

Split lines running upward

A split line that rises up and actually joins the Heart Line shows the affections exerted a strong influence over the mentality and that love ran away with the person's powers of rationalization. You sometimes see these lines followed by a definite change in the direction of the Head Line showing that love has completely altered the way in which the person thinks.

Split line rising to join the
Heart Line

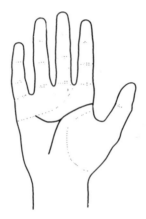

... and changing the direction
of the Head Line

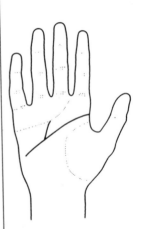

Split line merging with the
Head Line

● A split line that falls from the Heart Line and merges with the Head Line indicates that a difficult emotional decision has been made and was settled in favour of the Head. These decisions usually take some time to become final and although the initial decision is made when the line leaves the Heart line, the person is not able to live comfortably with the decision until the time the line merges with the Head Line.

● Split lines that droop from the Head Line show the pulling power of the imagination on the mentality. The person dreams and hopes, but because the Head Line continues on its original course he doesn't allow himself to follow those dreams and his hopes remain unfulfilled.

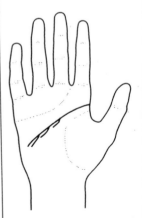

Split lines drooping from the
Head Line

Position of Head Line
The higher the set of the Head Line the more materialistic the basis upon which the person makes his decisions.

● A Head Line that is set very high on the hand shows a person wants a lot in life.
● When set low on the hand the person is more likely to be content with what he has and although he may like the idea of having all the good things in life, he has other priorities and won't make the sacrifices necessary to get them. If he is successful and finds he is able to afford all the luxuries, he will be very pleased, but this is a perk of being successful rather than the objective.

▶ **Timing of Events**

Use the same method as explained on p. 154, but remember that it is extremely difficult to date events and still largely a question of theory.

▶ **Active and Passive Hands**

When the Head Line is clearer and better marked in the active hand, it shows the person has learnt to make better use of his mentality, thinks more rationally and is more consistent in his decisions. People who have experienced financial difficulty in their lives often have a much straighter Head Line in their active hand showing they have had to learn to be more practical, level-headed and realistic. Those who have never had to worry about money often have a more sloping Head Line in their active hand indicating that as money was not a problem they were able to allow themselves to be more imaginative and idealistic.

THE LIFE LINE

*A*s a general rule the Life Line relates to the physical aspects of people's nature, but there are many subtleties involved and great care must always be taken when reading from this line. Not only does it show strength, health and physical vitality, it also shows the effect these matters have on the kind of life they live, the quality of that life and whether or not they are likely to have children.

The Life Line rises from the side of the hand between the Mounts of Jupiter and Lower Mars, curves around the Mount of Venus, and ends at the wrist. The longer the line, the longer the period in which they can expect to enjoy physical vitality and a strong constitution. The shorter the line, the shorter the period in which they can rely on physical vitality and the sooner they will have to depend on the careful husbanding of physical resources to continue living. An absent Life Line is quite unusual, but it indicates an absence of physical vitality, a lack of muscular strength, and also that the person survives mostly on nervous energy.

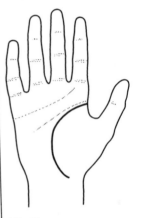

Life Line

Benham says a great deal about diagnosing specific illnesses from this and other lines in the hand. However, tremendous advances have been made in the field of medicine since he wrote his book and although periods of reduced physical vitality and possible sickness are marked on the lines, a reader should avoid trying to diagnose specific illnesses and refer his client to a medical specialist who is better equipped to diagnose and treat various physical ailments.

▶ The Length of the Line

Whereas the length of the Head and Heart Lines can give you a considerable amount of information regarding the nature of your subject, the actual length of the Life Line says little or nothing about the person as he is. Many people still believe that the Life Line relates to the length of a person's life and, unfortunately, when they see a long Life Line, many readers automatically jump to the conclusion that its owner is going to live a long and healthy life. But there are many subtleties involved and people with long Life Lines don't always live long lives, and those with short lines sometimes live to very great ages.

It is common for a palm reader to be consulted by someone who insists on knowing when he is going to die, but under no circumstances should any reader attempt to try to predict the length of life or time of death. There are far too many variables for any predictions about this to be relied on with certainty, and in matters as serious as this, a reader should avoid saying anything that he isn't absolutely certain about. In fact, the reader would be wiser to try to discover and deal with the anxieties or uncertainties that are motivating their client to be so concerned about the time of death.

▶ The Starting Point of the Line

The starting point of this line does not vary a great deal from hand to hand. There is, however, one variation you will occasionally see and this is when the line starts from the Mount of Jupiter. This adds great strength to the relative power of that mount and shows an extremely ambitious person who always tries to associate with those who are in higher positions than he is. As he is so willing to strive for his goals, this person is likely to be very successful.

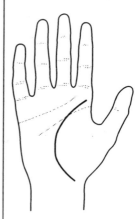

Starting on Jupiter

▶ The Sweep of the Line

The greater the outward curve or sweep of the line, the greater the strength and physical vitality of the individual.

A wide sweep

If the line sweeps well out into the hand it shows a person who has so much strength and physical vitality that their physical system is able to withstand a considerable amount of abuse and overindulgence before showing any ill effects. This type of line is often seen on those who are constantly out and about enjoying themselves, but unfortunately, because they have so much strength and vitality, they wear others out quickly and find there are very few who can keep up with them.

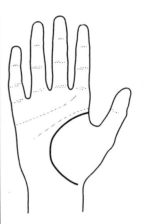

Wide sweep

Curving around Venus

A line that simply curves around the Mount of Venus is a more normal condition and shows a good amount of strength and physical vitality.

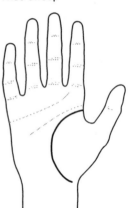

Curving around Venus

Running over Venus

If the line runs close to the thumb and over the Mount of Venus, it shows someone who lacks both muscular strength and physical vitality. He runs out of energy quickly and when forced to exert himself physically, tires easily. He consequently doesn't do well in occupations that require physical strength and prefers sedentary or non-strenuous forms of work. As he lacks vitality he is not sexually very active and is unlikely to marry early. He is also unlikely to have children because being aware of the fact that he lacks strength, he avoids courses of action that may result in situations that are too much for him to cope with. The more the line cuts

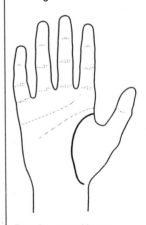

Running over Venus

in on the Mount of Venus, the more his lack of vitality restricts his life and the quieter his lifestyle is likely to be.

Close to the thumb

If the line runs very close to the thumb a person's physical system is unable to withstand any strain and they will need a great deal of rest and sleep. If with this indication the consistency of the hand is elastic, they will be active in only light or non-strenuous ways.

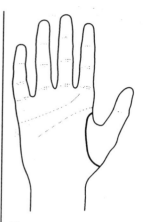
Close to the thumb

▶ The Ending of the Line

The quality of the Life Line generally weakens and grows thinner towards its end indicating the diminishing strength of the physical energies. However, a weakening of a line that drops straight to the wrist is not as serious as one that curves back towards the thumb.

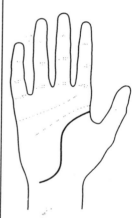
Dropping to Luna

● A line that stretches out across the hand and ends on the Mount of Luna shows a very restless disposition and a person who has such a strong desire to travel he will find it almost impossible to settle down to any routine kind of life.

● A line that runs around the Mount of Venus and then drops straight to the wrist shows a strong constitution and someone who is likely to retain his vitality to the end of his days.

● A line that begins to curve back onto the Mount of Venus shows diminishing vitality in later years. Although the person may be out and about, he will need a great deal of rest.

● A line that fragments and gives the appearance of a tassel shows the energies will dissipate themselves and the person will be prey to all sorts of illnesses in old age.

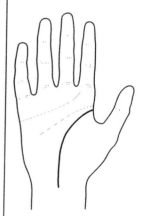
Dropping to the wrist

● If the line ends before it has run its full course the person should be advised to take care of his health and monitor it regularly. The point at which the line ends shows the age after which he will live on nervous energy and no longer be able to rely on reserves of physical strength. If a short line ends in a dot, crossbar or tassel it is a very serious matter and the person should be advised to have frequent medical check-ups.

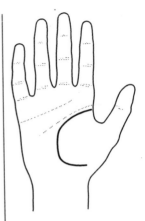

Line running back to Venus

▶ General Information

Character of the line

The depth and clarity of the line is important to observe. Look out for the changes in the line that indicate the changes a person has undergone.

● A line that is deep, clear and even shows your subject has a great deal of physical vitality and lives a rewarding life, even if the outward sweep of the line is not great.
● A broad and shallow line shows diminished vitality and although the person may go to work and spend his leisure time doing things he enjoys, he will not find life rewarding.
● A thin line shows someone who cannot endure a great deal of hardship and who tires easily when trying to exert himself physically.

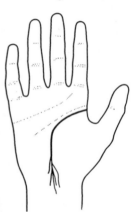

Fragmented line

When the line is poorly marked or uneven, the person is prone to worrying and often just doesn't feel well. When you see a weak line it is important to check for fluted nails as the tendency to feel stressed or worried often springs from the fact that the person tires easily and fears getting involved in situations that are too much for him to cope with.

● A dot on the line normally relates to health

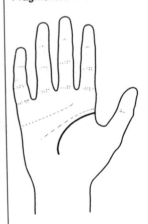

Line ending early

matters and shows difficulty at the time at which it appears. It interrupts the energy flow and the deeper or more clearly it is marked, the more serious the indications.

• An island shows a division of the energies and a period of difficulty in life. The person is unsettled and although an island often follows a defect such as a dot, showing that the health has been weakened by illness, it sometimes indicates the person simply feels run-down and is unable to make the effort to get his life organized.

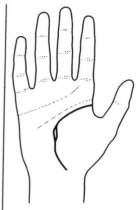

Island

• A chain shows extended periods of difficulty that relate either to the person's health or to the quality of his life. When the line suddenly gets very deep it shows a period of great stress and strain.

• A laddered line shows a weak physical constitution. The person lacks vitality and should be advised to avoid stressful situations. His energy levels are intermittent and unstable and he will tire easily. If Venus is developed he may have a strong desire for sex and fantasize a great deal, but he lacks the vitality he needs to turn his desires into reality. Many people with weak, thin or laddered Life Lines have difficulty finding their ideal mates. They want sex, but they don't want too much and so often refrain from getting involved in case they are unable to cope with what is expected of them.

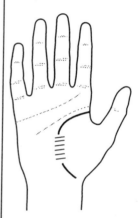

Laddered lines

• A break in the Life Line is serious and shows a break in the natural energy flow. Although often the result of illness or accident, this is not always the case as a break sometimes corresponds with a complete change in the life or lifestyle of the individual. If the break is accompanied by a sister or repair line the person is protected from the worst effects of this indication.

Any tendency of the line to turn back towards its source after a break is very serious and has always been considered to be a mark of fatality. But although this is theoretically quite reasonable, it is

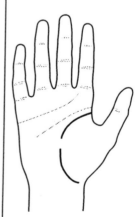

Broken

rare to see this on a hand and consequently difficult
to verify.

Change of direction
Should the line undergo a slight change of direction
it will indicate a change in lifestyle.

● If it suddenly starts to adopt a greater outward
curve the lifestyle is more active.
● If it suddenly begins to curve in on the Mount
of Venus the lifestyle is less active and more
restricted.

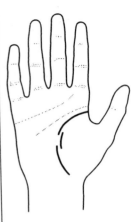

Repair lines

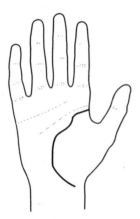

Greater outward curve

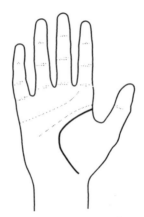

Restricted curve

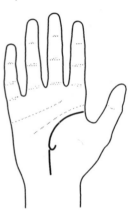

Line turned back

Energy lines
What are known as energy lines sometimes leave
the Life Line and rise up towards one of the
mounts. These lines are always good to see as they
show the person makes considerable efforts to
improve himself or achieve a particular goal. On a
hand with soft consistency they indicate he strives
to overcome his inherent laziness and, in so far as
his particular goal is concerned, he makes a great
deal of effort. Sometimes these lines are just short,
but they can rise to a mount.

- If a line rises to Jupiter it shows the person makes an effort to rise and improve both himself and his status in life. The time at which the effort is made is marked by the time the energy line leaves the Life Line.
- Should the line rise to Saturn it shows he makes a considerable effort to increase his financial security and material well-being. If there is no Saturn Line on the hand then an energy line rising to Saturn will often substitute for one.
- Many successful people who don't have particularly strong thumbs have a number of these little lines showing they achieve their success through continued spurts of effort rather than willpower, perception, and long-range planning. The condition of the Life Line after one of these energy lines should always be carefully examined as sometimes the person works too hard for his objectives and undermines his health and reserves of energy.

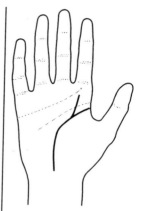

To Jupiter

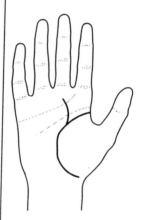

To Saturn

Colour

- Pink does a lot to reduce the severity of any defects in the line.
- Red is also good and increases the intensity of the physical vitality.
- White shows physical lethargy, even when the line is well marked.

 Timing of Events

The dating of events on this line is similar to dating of events on the Head and Heart Lines except that instead of measuring the actual length of the line, you should measure the normal distance it is expected to travel. Use small dividers set to 1 centimetre and measure from the lines

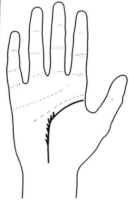

Little lines

beginning, around the Mount of Venus, and down to the wrist. If it ends early you must simply follow its expected course. The measurement from start to wrist covers seventy years of life and by setting the dividers to ten-year intervals you can work your way through the line a decade at a time.

▶ Active and Passive Hands

If the Life Line in the active hand is not as well marked as the line in the passive hand, the person has not been taking care of his health. A line that is better marked in the active hand shows the physical constitution is stronger and more resistant to disease than it was.

THE FATE LINE

*A*lthough it has generally been accepted that the Fate line (sometimes called the Saturn Line) shows the events of life, many readers experience great difficulty when trying to relate the reality of a person's life to the course and condition of the line. It is not that the traditional meaning is completely wrong, but the indications of this line are more complex, and many subtleties have been overlooked. What the Fate Line does show is the directional attitude of the individual and how that attitude is affected by events. For instance, the presence of a Fate Line will show the person has direction in life and goals towards which to work, but when it is badly marked or defective in any way it will show he is experiencing difficulty and failing to make the kind of progress he would like to make. This is a very valuable line when considering a person's relationship towards his direction in life and what he works to achieve. If clear and well marked, it indicates he finds satisfaction in what he is doing and feels that he is making progress in life. However, if this line is absent, it shows he has no direction in life and exists rather than lives. He is like a ship without a rudder and, as he doesn't know where his efforts will eventually lead him, he gets very little satisfaction from any work that he does do.

▶ The Starting Point of the Line

The starting point of this line will show the attitude of the individual when he first started to find a direction or purpose in his life. As any career is normally a progressive series of events, this early attitude is important to consider because it is likely to shape his whole future.

From the Mount of Luna

If the Fate Line starts from the Mount of Luna on the passive side of the hand, it indicates that in the early part of his career the person allowed things to happen and tended to go along with the opportunities that came his way. It has often been suggested that this line shows someone whose career was helped by outside influences or a person of the opposite sex, but as his passive directional attitude inclined him to go along with the trend of events, should another person have offered to assist him in any way he would have responded to their ideas and, if reasonable, gone along with their suggestions.

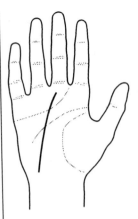

From Luna

From the centre of the hand

If starting from the centre of the hand, it shows the person's attitude to his career was equally balanced between the active and passive sides of his nature. He followed his own desires about his direction in life, but was willing to respond to the trend of events, opportunities that came his way, or any help others may have offered.

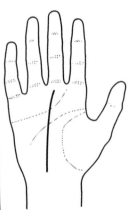

From the centre

From the Life Line

If starting from the Life Line it indicates the person was self-motivated in his choice of career or direction in life and his early course was dictated by his own personal desires. As the line starts from the Life Line it also shows he put a lot of energy into getting his life together and then worked to maintain his course or balance. Unlike a person with a line starting on Luna the early part of his career depended on his own efforts rather than the trend of events or help from others.

From inside the Life Line

A Fate Line starting from inside the Life Line is

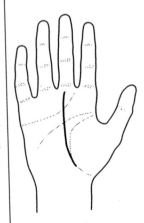

From the Life Line

quite rare and has generally been considered to show that the person's career or direction in life was greatly influenced or helped by his family. However, because it is such a rare indication this interpretation has been difficult to verify.

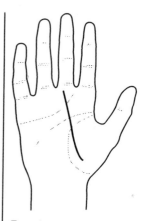

From inside the Life Line

From low on the hand

A line that starts low on the hand is normally centrally located and indicates the person was aware of his direction or course in life when he was still very young. Consequently, during his early years he would have made decisions and chosen courses of action that were based on what he perceived his future was going to be.

Normal

Normally the line doesn't start until some way into the hand showing that in youth such persons left many decisions to their parents or guardians and tended not to think about their direction in life. From the time they left home to the time the line starts their life would have lacked cohesion and they would have existed rather than lived. They may have worked, but the job was just a job and did not give any sense of purpose or direction in life. From the time the line starts they would have begun to find some direction and been able to tailor their actions to what they wanted to do or achieve in the future.

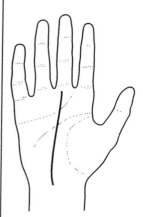

From low on the hand

From high in the hand

A line that doesn't start until well up in the hand is sometimes associated with minor defects in the Head Line showing that as the person lacked clarity of thought he was unable to develop any sense of purpose or direction in life.

Often a line that begins high in the hand rises

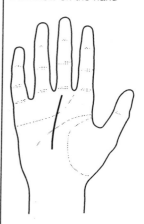

Normal

from the Life Line showing that after going
through a long period of just existing in life, the
person began to make considerable efforts to
collect himself and develop some purpose or
direction.

From very high in the hand

If the line doesn't start until very high up in the
hand it shows the person lacked any sense of
purpose or direction until much later in life. I have
seen this a few times on people who tended to
follow the crowd in their youth and do whatever
their friends did. Although not family minded,
when their friends got married they got married
and because of the consequent responsibilities
they were unable to develop their lives along
desired lines. Then, when their children had
grown up and left home they finally found the
freedom to do things that gave their lives some
sense of direction.

Absence of the Fate Line

A hand that has no Fate Line has often been
considered to show a self-made person and
someone who has to rely on his own efforts to get
anywhere. But this is not quite correct as a
complete absence of the line shows the person's life
lacks any cohesion, purpose or direction. He drifts
through life and exists rather than lives. Although
he may be financially successful there is nothing
in his life that is meaningful enough to point him
in a particular direction. Consequently, there is
never any purpose behind the work that he does
do and whatever his successes they give him
no inner satisfaction or sense of progression in
life. He is unlikely to feel that his life is really
worthwhile.

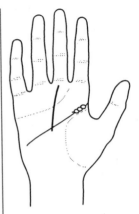

From high up

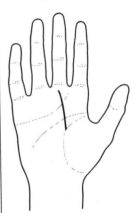

Rising from the Life Line

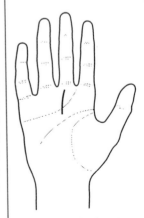

From very high up

▶ The Course of the Line Through the Hand

The Fate Line should normally lie in the centre of the hand indicating a balance between the person's inner desires and outside influences.

- If it lies on the passive side of the hand, the person's direction in life is overly dependent on the trend of events and outside influences.
- Should it lie on the active side of the hand, their direction is the result of their own actions, but their desire to maintain a particular course in life means that they have to impose limitations and refrain from responding to the influences of other people, the trend of events, or opportunities that might come their way.
- If the line starts on Luna and then takes a more central position on the hand, they depended on influences and the trend of events in the earlier part of life. However, as they have grown older, they have gained more balance between their inner desires and outer influences.

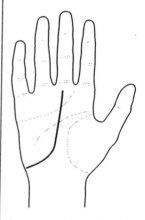

Starting on Luna, becoming central

- A line that starts from the Life Line and then moves towards the passive side of the hand shows the person started by making personal efforts to get his life together, but as he grew older he began to allow himself to become overly dependent on outside influences and events.
- It is not uncommon to see the early part of the line running close to the Life Line and then a break, with the remainder of the line situated in the centre of the hand. In such a case the early part of the person's life was motivated by his own personal efforts, but limited or restricted by where he wanted to go and what he wanted to do. At a later date he underwent a change of attitude, became more balanced and more willing to allow outside influences or events to affect his direction in life. This type of line is sometimes seen on

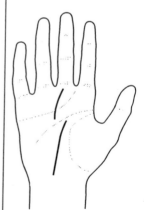

Break in the line

people who restricted themselves and devoted the first part of their lives to their family and bringing up their children, but once they had achieved their initial goal they started to let themselves go and became more receptive to outside influences and events.

▶ The Ending of the Line

The Mount of Saturn is the normal ending place for the Fate Line.

A line that stops before it has run its full course indicates that at the point where it stops the person ceases to have any purpose or direction in life. A complete stop to the line before it has run its full course is unusual and more often than not it is simply a case of the line becoming much weaker or thinner. In such persons this indicates that the sense of purpose diminishes and they cease to pay a great deal of attention to the direction of their life. It is quite usual for the line to be very strong in the earlier part of the hand and considerably weaker in the later part indicating that direction was very important during their earlier years and they worked hard to develop their life along desired lines. Once they achieved a certain point they slowed down, content simply to maintain their position. The point at which they slowed down is indicated by the point at which the line loses its strength and becomes weaker or thinner.

Sometimes the main line comes to an end and there are a variety of small, thin lines on the mount of Saturn. Such persons cease to concentrate their efforts into a single direction and spread their energies across a wide field. This indication is the same as a number of vertical lines on the Mount of Saturn showing that in later life a variety of things are important, and they try to maintain each.

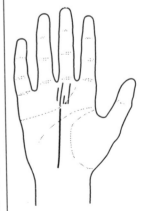

Small lines on Saturn

If the line goes to Jupiter it shows that in later life they do more than just maintain their direction in life, they achieve some very important goals.

If the line goes to Apollo it shows that in later life the ability to relax and enjoy life (Apollo) is more important than security (Saturn). Great riches in later life have often been attributed to a Fate Line that ends on Apollo, and it is true that if people come into a great deal of money they are likely to spend it indulgently. But this ending may also be a result of finding the need for security diminishing as they grow older and then starting to spend their savings on simply enjoying themselves.

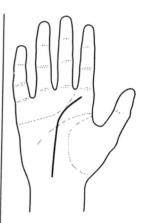

Line rising to Jupiter

▶ General Information

Character of the line

The character of the line frequently changes as it progresses up the hand and each change reflects a change to the quality of the person's career or direction in life.

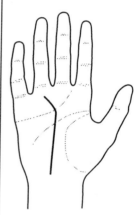

Line rising to Apollo

- If the line is clear and well marked, it shows that from a work point of view, life is going well and the subject feels he is making progress.
- If broad and shallow, it shows a person struggling in life, finding it difficult to make headway and dissatisfied with the course of events.
- An island shows a time of great difficulty and that the person will be divided and unsettled.
- A chain shows an extended period of great difficulty.
- Sections of the line that are very deep show periods of great struggles and stresses in a person's career or direction in life.
- A crossbar is a negative sign and shows an interference to the natural direction of life. If followed by a weakening or thinning of the line, it indicates

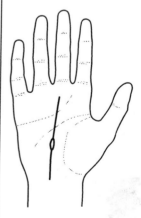

Island

the interference causes the person to lose momentum and interest in maintaining his direction. It is
not unusual to see a crossbar followed by a weakening of the line, which in turn is followed by a
break. In such a case, the interference has caused a
loss of interest and momentum, which in turn is
followed by a temporary loss of direction or a
change. If the new line is placed differently the
change may well result in a change of job or career,
but it need not necessarily do so. For instance an
architect works in a company (hypothetically
speaking), has a major setback (crossbar), loses his
momentum and interest in what he is doing (weakening line), develops new interests and starts
working towards new goals (new line in new direction). He may still work in the same company and
do the same job, but his direction is different and
the goals he works towards are also different.
Consequently, as a result of his changed attitude he
will be responding to a different set of values and
his life will begin to develop along different lines.
The actual interference occurs at the time of the
crossbar and any consequent changes to the line
show the effects of that interference. The deeper
the crossbar the greater the interference, but sometimes there is no change to the character of the line
showing the person has been able to cope with the
difficulty.

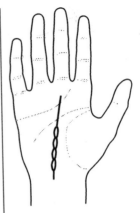

Chain

• A dot in the line has a similar meaning to a crossbar and shows a period of sudden, unexpected
difficulty. The condition of the line after the dot
will show how it affected the direction or career of
the individual. If the line peters out and doesn't
reappear then it has had very serious consequences
and the person never manages to regain a direction
to his life.

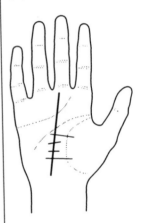

Crossbars

Break

A break is a serious matter.

● If the line just stops and then starts again a short time later it shows the person loses his direction for a period of time.

● If the new line is placed differently on the hand or goes in a different direction then there is a complete change in the directional attitude of the individual.

● If the lines overlap then the change is a gradual one which begins at the time the new line starts and becomes final when the old one finishes.

● If there is no overlapping of the lines then the change is sudden and perhaps even unexpected.

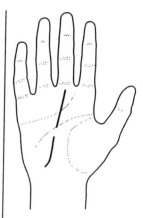

Restarting, same position

It is quite common to see the line growing weaker before a break, showing that the person loses his momentum and any interest he had in his direction before undergoing a change. But when dealing with breaks in the Fate Line it is, however, important to remember that a change of attitude is generally the result of something that happens in life. A person who finds his direction meaningful and is enjoying some degree of success is unlikely to feel any need to change his attitude, whereas someone who is experiencing problems or difficulties in his life is much more likely to reconsider his position and alter or change his directional attitude or what he wants to do in life.

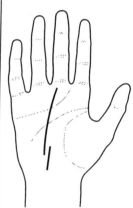

Differently placed

Offshoot

● An offshoot or branch line rising from the Fate Line and going towards the Mount of Apollo shows the person's idea of his success is considerably enhanced, but the kind of success depends very much on his personal sense of values. If he gauges his degree of success in life by his assets and how

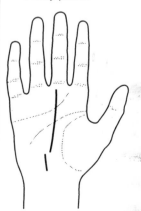

Different direction

much money he has in the bank then an offshoot
will show an increase in wealth. If he is a home-
loving person then an offshoot may show that
improvements in his family life make him feel
richer. If he is a priest he may find he is more
successful in his efforts to convert the masses or
help the needy.

● Should the line rise towards Jupiter it shows an
increase in status or authority, and that the person
has a greater ability to influence others or control
events. These branch lines are often only short
showing a short period of increased success, but if
they are long and rise to the mount then the period
of increased success is long lasting.

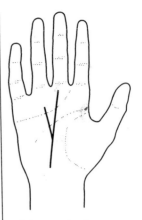

Offshoot to Apollo

Extra lines

● A small line joining the Fate Line shows the individual's directional attitude was influenced by
another person. These influence lines sometimes
show marriage, sometimes a business partnership,
and sometimes just that another person has had a
great influence on the direction he decided to take
in life.

● Should the Fate Line undergo a change of direction immediately after an influence line joins it then
the influence has altered the directional attitude of
the individual. After the join the condition of the
Fate Line must always be carefully observed as this
will tell you whether the influence has had a
beneficial or detrimental effect.

● An influence line that fails to join the Fate Line
and just runs up alongside it shows the influence
gives a great deal of assistance to the person's career
or direction in life, but doesn't actually become a
part of that direction as would happen in the case of
a business partnership or marriage.

● It is common to see a weak Fate Line, which
grows considerably clearer and stronger after being

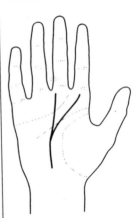

Offshoot to Jupiter

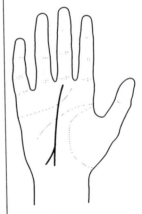

Influence Line

joined by an influence line. This is often a sign of marriage showing that the union gave the person some real purpose and sense of direction in life.

Other Features

In the later part of the hand, normally just after it crosses the Head Line, the Fate Line frequently grows thinner or weaker showing that after a certain age the person began to lose interest in maintaining his direction in life or pursuing his career. A thinning or weakening of this line is also often seen on people who inherit large amounts of money showing that once they had become wealthy, career and direction were no longer as important to them as before the inheritance.

When compared to the other lines on the hand, the stronger the proportional strength of the Fate Line the more the person is interested in pursuing his career and maintaining his direction in life. A deep, well-marked Fate Line that runs straight to the Mount of Saturn and is not joined by any influence lines shows a person to whom career and direction are all important, and who is consequently quite lonely in life. He concentrates so much on what he is doing and where he wants to go that he ignores other equally important aspects of his life. Anything that interferes with his direction or slows his progress is avoided, and that includes marriage and meaningful friendships. If he does get married his marriage will always take second place to his career, and if there is a conflict of interest, career and direction will win out, even if that means breaking up the marriage.

Grill

• A grill on the Mount of Saturn is a bad sign, even when the Fate Line is clear and well marked. In

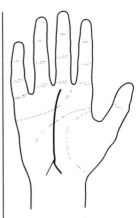

Joined influence line

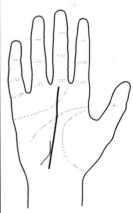

Unjoined influence line

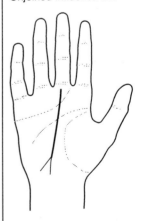

Influence line strengthening Fate Line

such a case the person has direction and purpose in life, but the progress he makes is likely to be very inconsistent and he will never do as well as he hopes.

Hollow

● A noticeable hollow in the centre of the hand has often been said to show bad luck in material matters. But the hollow is the result of a deficient Plain of Mars showing the person doesn't like to make a fuss. Unfortunately, if people don't make a fuss and stand up for themselves when they should, difficult situations are likely to develop, which will, in turn, make it considerably more difficult for them to be successful in life. Even if strong willed and intelligent, they become victims of their own easygoing nature and unwillingness to shout out and complain about any injustice they may be subjected to. (An employer or manager who is looking for someone to work overtime without pay will almost always first approach the person who is least likely to complain about being asked.) If the deepest part of the hollow lies close to the Life Line then the person experiences difficulty or bad luck in his personal or home life for the same reasons.

▶ Timing of Events

Because there is no curve to the Fate Line the timing of events is considerably easier than on other lines. The distance from the apex of the Mount of Saturn to the base of the palm (normally, though not always, the top bracelet) is seventy years. Once you have measured that distance you can, as with the other lines, use a small pair of dividers to work your way up the line a decade at a time. (Length divided by seventy and multiplied by ten equals a distance of ten years.) Another effective way of determining the age of an event on this line is to determine the distance occupied by each year (length divided by seventy = one year). Then measure the distance from the apex of the Mount of Saturn to the point you are interested in, divide that measurement by the year figure, and then subtract your result from seventy. (Apex of Saturn to point of interest = distance. Distance divided by year = years from seventy. Seventy minus years from seventy = age of event.)

▶ Active and Passive Hands

If the line in the active hand is clearer and better marked than the one in the passive hand, it indicates the person has been more constructive in his approach to his career or direction in life and is consequently likely to experience a greater degree of success. He will also avoid many difficulties that might otherwise have beset him. If the line in the active hand is not as clear or well marked as the one in the passive, then the situation is simply reversed.

THE LINE OF APOLLO

*T*his is a difficult line to deal with and a great deal of confusion still surrounds its precise meaning. In the past it has generally been considered to show either great wealth and success, or great artistic ability, but as an Apollo line is often seen on the hands of those who are neither wealthy nor artistic, many readers are cautious when dealing with it. Unfortunately, one of the major problems is that as most hands don't have an Apollo line, opportunities for constructive research are limited.

Although this line does show wealth and success in life, the important thing to remember is that it shows success from the point of view of the individual and not from that of the world at large. Consequently, this can be considered to be a line of personal success and when seen on a hand it shows the person is able to live the life he wants to live and is also in a position to do things that are expressive of his individuality. For instance, an artist with this line will find that if not actually rich or successful, he can make a living by painting what he wants to paint whereas an artist without a line of Apollo will find himself having to draw or paint pictures which, rather than reflecting his individuality, are in keeping with what the public will buy or what others are paying him to do.

A housewife with this line will feel that her life is successful and will also find herself able to do the kind of things she personally wants to do. Someone who inherits a considerable amount of money will be able to live the lifestyle he wants to live and also do the things he wants to do. This is why an inheritance is often indicated by a thinning or weakening of the Fate line, which coincides with the appearance of an Apollo line. A mentally retarded person who is cared for in an institution may also have this line showing that as all his basic needs are cared for, he is able to spend his time indulgently, doing the things he likes doing.

People without a line of Apollo can and often do become extremely successful and may even receive international acclaim for their achievements. But in these cases, no matter how successful these people are and no matter how much satisfaction they get from their success, the absence of an Apollo line will show that they do not achieve the kind of success they would like to achieve and are therefore unable to live the kind of life they would like to live. On the other hand, a person who makes a modest living by doing what he wants to do is likely to feel personally successful and this personal success will be shown by the appearance of an Apollo line on the hand.

Benham refers to this line as the line of capability or brilliance, but it is, however, important to remember that although people who are very talented can normally achieve a high degree of success by doing the things they want to do, circumstances may allow someone who is not particularly talented to make his living by doing something that he really enjoys doing.

The starting point of the line

The starting point of the line will tell you the age at which feelings of personal success begin.

• Often this line doesn't start until quite high in the hand showing that it takes many years for the person to develop his life to the point where he can begin to feel personally successful.
• If, as sometimes happens, the line starts close to the wrist, then either through luck, circumstances, or personal talent the person begins to enjoy some form of personal success at an early age.
• Most frequently there is just a thin line starting very high on the hand showing that the person is

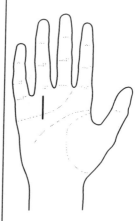

Apollo Line high up

only able to live the life he wants to live after retirement. A single vertical line on the Mount of Apollo, if clear and well marked, doubles as an Apollo line and although it strengthens the Apollonian characteristics considerably, no matter how artistic or individually creative the person is, because the line appears only on the Mount of Apollo, he will not achieve personal success until late in life.

▶ **General Information**

Character of the line

The deeper, clearer and better marked the line, the greater the degree of personal success the person can be expected to achieve. It is the comparative strength of this line that has to be carefully considered. In a case where the line is clear, well marked, and prominent the person can be expected to enjoy a considerable amount of personal success in life, so much so that some degree of notable fame or personal acclaim is likely. But most Apollo lines are comparatively weak or thin and show only a limited amount of personal success. Defects such as an island, dot or crossbar show times when the person's degree of personal success undergoes some form of difficulty.

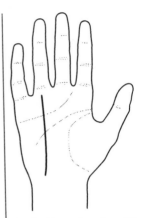

Apollo Line, close to wrist

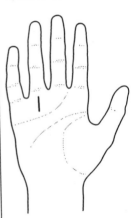

Single Line on Mount of Apollo

- An island shows an extended period of difficulty.
- A dot shows something sudden and unexpected.
- A crossbar shows some form of interference.
- A well-marked star on this line has always been considered to show great fame and success, but very few people achieve the kind of success and personal acclaim they wish to achieve and it is consequently a very unusual sign.

As with defects on any line, the quality of the Apollo Line after a defect must be carefully

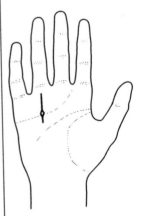

Island on Apollo

observed to see whether or not the difficulty has any long-lasting effects.

A link between the Fate and Apollo Lines

An Apollo Line can compensate for an absent Fate Line but does show that rather than considering their future and trying to develop their life along desired lines, such persons spend their time living for the present and doing what they enjoy doing.

For best results the Fate and Apollo Lines should be of equal strength as this shows that the strength of their desire to continue developing their life along desired lines (directional attitude) is matched by equally strong feelings of personal success.

● If the Apollo Line is stronger, then their desire to do the things they want to do and live the life they want to live is stronger than their desire to continue developing their life along desired lines.

● If the Fate Line is the stronger of the two, then although the desire to develop their life along desired lines is accompanied by some feelings of personal success, they do not feel as personally successful as they would like.

Timing of events

The system for dating events on the Apollo Line is the same as that used for dating events on the Fate Line. The distance from the apex of the Mount of Apollo to the base of the palm is seventy years and each mark or change to the character of the line can be calculated accordingly.

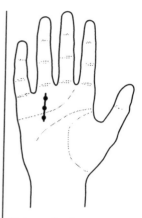

Dots on Apollo

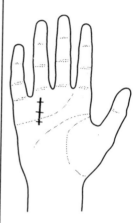

Crossbars on Apollo

MINOR LINES OF
THE HAND

▶ The Line of Mercury

This is sometimes called the line of health.
However, as most palmists are not qualified doctors
they will not have a clear understanding of all the
various illnesses this line is reputed to indicate.

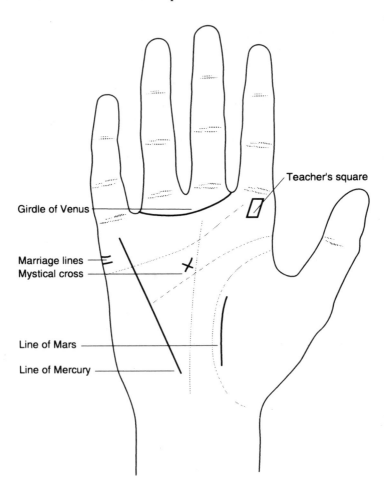

Consequently, a reader who sees defects such as islands, dots or crossbars on this line should refrain from trying to diagnose a specific illness and refer the subject to a doctor for a medical check-up.

Despite what has been said in the past this line is far from being understood and the general rule of thumb for a student to follow is that a person who does not have a line of Mercury in his hand is likely to enjoy better health than someone who has one that is wavy or defectively marked in some way.

▶ The Girdle of Venus

Some authors describe this line as an extra Heart Line and say that it shows a very emotional person. But more realistically a Girdle of Venus shows a highly strung nature and someone who is prone to nervous tension. Should the Mounts of Luna or Saturn be strongly developed then the nervous tension is likely to be particularly pronounced. If the subject also has fluted nails, this condition will be still more serious.

▶ The Line of Mars

Not to be confused with influence lines, this line runs alongside the Life Line but is completely separate from it. It adds strength to the Life Line and is normally seen on people who have an abundance of physical energy. However, when found on a soft or flabby hand this excess of energy is likely to be expended in the pursuit of pleasure.

▶ Influence Lines

These are small branch lines that leave the Life Line and either run alongside it or else run onto the

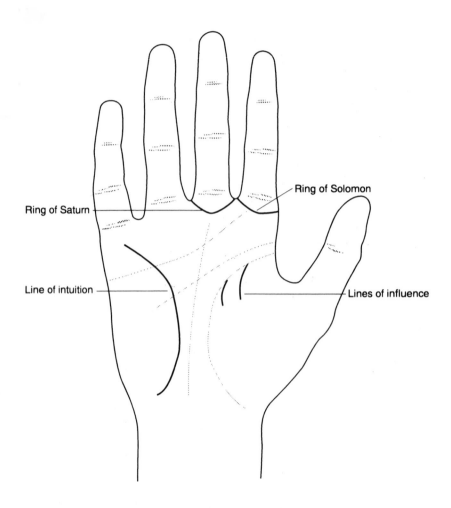

Mount of Venus. Normally considered to show love relationships, there is some confusion regarding whether the person on whose hand the influence line appears is the active or passive participant. (Does he care for the influence or does the influence care for him?) As an influence line is a split line which leaves the Life Line and draws energy from it, the indications are that the person cares for someone and this caring creates an energy drain or causes some form of restriction to life.

If the influence line runs close to the Life Line then although the influence causes an energy drain he/she also acts as a supportive influence. However, if the line moves away from the Life Line and runs onto the Mount of Venus then the influence drains the person of energy and does not give back as much as is given.

The stronger the proportional strength of the influence line, the greater the energy drain and the more the person cares for the influence. The quality and condition of the Life Line after a strong influence line leaves it should be carefully observed, especially when the line runs onto the Mount of Venus as any defects in the Life Line can often be attributed, at least in part, to the draining effect of the influence line.

▶ The Ring of Saturn

This line is a defective mark on the Mount of Saturn and shows that the person cannot respond to his instinct for security and is consequently unable to be successful at anything. No matter how much he wants to succeed on a conscious level, a deep-seated or subconscious desire to fail prevents him from achieving any of his goals. He either sets his ambitions unrealistically high or, at the moment of success, he allows some minor incident to stand in his way and prevent him from achieving his aims.

▶ Line of Intuition

This indicates an energy flow between the Mounts of Mercury and Luna and shows the person has an instinctive feeling for the true nature of those he comes into contact with. Without quite knowing how he does it, he will find that he can instantly sense other people's real mood and tell whether or not they are sincere in what they are saying. It is not generally an ability he is consciously aware of, but when lied to, even by an expert in the art of deception, he automatically begins to feel uncomfortable or uneasy.

▶ The Teacher's Square

Reputed to show talent as a teacher, the major problem with this and other minor lines on the hand is that there is, as yet, no clear understanding of the psychological disposition that would incline a person towards a particular career. In this case, as the square is found on the Mount of Jupiter it strengthens the desire for control and consequently indicates that the person wishes to be influential and impress his or his society's ideas and beliefs on other people. As teaching is one of the most effective ways of achieving this aim, it is quite reasonable to expect a number of teachers to have this mark on their hand.

▶ The Ring of Solomon

Traditionally this line was reputed to show someone who was a master in one of the occult sciences, but more modern authors have tended to refer to it as showing a talent for psychology. However, the psychological inclinations that would result in a person becoming interested in psychology or one of the occult sciences are presently not understood.

As many people develop an interest in the occult because they are looking for something and many good psychologists initially took up their profession because they were aware of their own psychological deficiencies, it is theoretically possible that this line indicates some kind of psychological or emotional difficulty that relates to the Jupiterian desires for dominance or control.

▶ The Mystical Cross

Although this is reputed to show someone who has a great interest in occult or mystical studies, there is presently no understanding of the psychological idiosyncrasies indicated by this mark.

▶ Marriage Lines

Many palmists have found the traditional meanings of these lines very unreliable and have ceased to refer to them when seeking information regarding their client's love life. Different people get married for different reasons and consequently a palmist must first be able to establish why his client will get married before he will know which part of the hand to look in.

Although there are many instances when marriage lines co-relate accurately with actual marriages, there are also many instances when the realities of the person's past life do not match the number of marriage lines on his hand. As they are found on Mercury, the mount of communication, these lines show the person communicates with someone in a very special way. The stronger the line the stronger the degree of communication and a deep, clearly marked line will show a very intimate relationship, but determining whether the association is of the marital kind, sexual or just platonic can be extremely difficult.

Most people are sensitive about their love life and although they may be happy to tell you when they got married, they may not be keen to discuss personal details such as affairs they might have had or people they loved and cared for but chose not to get involved with. Consequently, this is a very difficult line to research and as there are so many complexities to an intimate relationship, it must be handled with great caution.

202 THE LINES OF THE HAND

▶ Children Lines

These lines are extremely unreliable, so much so that most competent palmists now ignore them completely. Although there are occasions when on the hand of an older person the number of children lines accurately reflect the number of children he or she has had, these instances are rare. The accumulation of knowledge is an ongoing process and in time new information is likely to allow a palmist to deal with the question of children more accurately, but for the present it is wiser for the student to refrain from trying to use these lines to predict the number of children a person will have.

▶ Assorted Lines

A single vertical line on the top phalanx of any finger greatly increases the intellectual inclinations of the mind, especially in regard to the aspects indicated by the finger.

A single vertical line on the first or top phalanx of the thumb adds great strength to the willpower and character of the individual. This line is always good to see on thumbs that are proportionally short or weak on the hand.

COLLECTING PALM PRINTS

*C*ollecting palm prints is the most effective way of keeping a record of the hands you have read and by filing them alphabetically in ring binders you will find it very easy to check back and refresh your memory on points of interest. For instance, you may sometimes hear of a client who has got married, become very successful or emigrated to another country. By having a record of the lines on his hand you will be able to check back and see whether or not the markings on the hand accurately reflected the subsequent trend of events. Also, should you be consulted by the same person at a later date you will be in a position to check for changes to the quality or condition of individual lines.

To take prints you need a 10- or 15-cm (4- or 6-inch) rubber roller, which can be bought from any good art supplies shop, and some fingerprint ink, which can be obtained from Reeves, Middlesex, HA3 5RH, England. I differ from many other authors in my preference for fingerprint ink, which, although messier and more difficult to wash off than a water-based printer's ink, does give better results. You will also need a small plate of glass, a pencil with an adjustable lead (available from most stationers), some white photocopying paper and an old newspaper. Place a sheet of photocopying paper on the newspaper, put some ink on the plate of glass and use the roller to spread it as evenly as possible. Next, take your subject's hand and use the roller to cover it with a smooth film of ink and then place it on the photocopying paper. Use the pencil to draw in the outline of the hand and then carefully press down on the fingers and back of the palm. To make sure the lines on the whole palm are faithfully reproduced keep the hand steady, slide the newspaper off the table and press gently up into the centre of the palm with your fingers. After you have done this carefully remove the paper from the palm and repeat the procedure with the other hand. Cleaning is simply a matter of getting your subject to wash his hands with a good quality washing-up liquid and an added spoonful of sugar to act as an abrasive. A cloth dipped in kerosene can be used to clean the printing equipment.

Taking photographs is another effective way of keeping records but it is expensive, and, as some of the finer lines don't always show up, photographic records should only be used in conjunction with palm prints. What type of camera you should use depends on how much you can afford, but as good photography is an acquired skill and requires a great deal of practice, it would be advisable for the student to take a course in the subject before deciding on what equipment to purchase.

CHECK-LIST FOR LINES OF THE HAND

*T*his check-list deals with aspects that relate to the lines on the hand. Like the check-list at the end of Part I, it should be used to make sure each point is observed before you commit yourself to any statement. The check-list includes some lines that are not clearly understood at present, but I have done this in the hope that if you make a point of looking at each hand to see whether or not they are there, you may be able to discover exactly what they do mean.

To be completed for both left and right hands.

	Left	**Right**
1 Strongest line on the hand (?)		
Heart Line		
2 Length of line	_____	_____
3 Starting point of line	_____	_____
4 Quality of line	_____	_____
5 Changes of character or direction	_____	_____
6 Breaks or defects on line	_____	_____
Head Line		
7 Length of line	_____	_____
8 Starting point of line	_____	_____
9 Ending point of line	_____	_____
10 Sweep of line	_____	_____
11 Quality of line	_____	_____

12 Changes of character or direction   _____   _____
13 Breaks or defects in line   _____   _____

Life Line
14 Length of Line   _____   _____
15 Starting point of line   _____   _____
16 Ending point of line   _____   _____
17 Sweep of line   _____   _____
18 Quality of line   _____   _____
19 Changes of character or direction   _____   _____
20 Breaks or defects on line   _____   _____

Fate Line
21 Overall character of line   _____   _____
22 Starting point of line   _____   _____
23 Ending point of line   _____   _____
24 Changes of character or direction   _____   _____
25 Offshoots, breaks or defects   _____   _____

Line of Apollo (if present)
26 Overall character of line   _____   _____
27 Starting point of line   _____   _____
28 Ending point of line   _____   _____
29 Changes of character or direction   _____   _____
30 Breaks or defects on line   _____   _____

31 **Line of Mercury (if present)**   _____   _____
32 **Girdle of Venus (if present)**   _____   _____
33 **Line of Mars (if present)**   _____   _____
34 **Influence Lines (if present)**   _____   _____
35 **Ring of Saturn (if present)**   _____   _____
36 **Line of Intuition (if present)**   _____   _____
37 **Teacher's Square (if present)**   _____   _____
38 **Ring of Solomon (if present)**   _____   _____
39 **Mystical Cross (if present)**   _____   _____
40 **Marriage Lines (if present)**   _____   _____
41 **Children Lines (if present)**   _____   _____

RECOMMENDED READING

Altman, Nathaniel – *The Palmistry Workbook*, Aquarian Press, 1984

Benham, William G. – *The Laws of Scientific Hand Reading*, Hawthorn, New York, 1946

Brandon-Jones, David – *Practical Palmistry*, Hutchinson, London, 1981

Cheiro – *Language of the Hand*, Arrow Books, London, 1986

Cheiro – *Complete Palmistry*, Dell Publishing, New York, 1968

Cheiro – *You and Your Hand* (Revised by Louise Owen), Jarrolds, London, 1969

Fitzherbert, Andrew – *Hand Psychology*, Angus & Robertson, Australia, 1986

Holtzman, Arnold – *Applied Handreading*, Greenwood Chase Press, Toronto, 1983

Jaquin, Noel – *Practical Palmist*, D.B. Taraporevala Sons, India, 1984